Bangernomics Bible

GW00673562

How to Buy and Run a Car for Less

James Ruppert

The Front

Welcome to the wonderful world of buying and owning cars but with a twist, and that twist is called Bangernomics. Remember to strap yourself in; it could be a bumpy ride.

The Bangernomics Code

Bangernomics contrasts the absurd expense of buying new, with the supreme good sense of buying used.

Bangernomics will show the mechanically bewildered how to buy a safe, durable car and most important of all save money.

Bangernomics is all about motoring at the blunt end.

Bangernomics means never having to be fussy about what you drive.

Bangernomics defines no-nonsense motoring in the new millennium.

Bangernomics is a way of life, but remember, always beware of the dog.

Bangernomics

𝕭ible

How to Buy and Run a Car for Less

James Ruppert

FORESIGHT PUBLICATIONS

© James Ruppert 1993 to 2010 ©Action Automotive
Limited/Foresight Publications 2010

First published in 2010 by Foresight Publications, part of
Action Automotive Limited.

More information at:

www.bangernomics.com
www.foresightpublications.com
www.jamesruppert.co.uk

A CIP catalogue record for this book is available from the
British Library

ISBN 978–0–9559529–1–3

Printed and bound in Great Britain

Contents

Also by James Ruppert

The British Car Industry Our Part in its Downfall

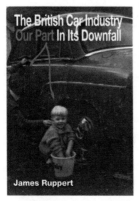

The true story of what happened to the British Car Industry from 1945 until it effectively ended with the implosion of MG Rover in 2005. It occurred to me that my Dad's car owning, driving and buying history (from a Triumph Mayflower to a VW Golf) was a great way of injecting some social history into it all. I also wondered whether his decision in the 1970s to buy an Audi triggered the downfall, or was it the inept motor industry management, stupid unions or meddling governments. I think we know the answer, but it is fun finding out and there some good stories along the way. There are also tons of small black and white pictures of cars and people from the era, plus all the cars that my Dad bought. Many of the cars featured have become Bangernomics legends. Essentially you do not need to be a petrolhead to enjoy it. Also reviewers have said very nice things.

Beautifully written with considerable wit. Honest John – Daily Telegraph

We're big fans of Ruppert's writing ... it's a great read. Highly Recommended – Dep-O Magazine

A light emotive and charming view of a difficult period for British pride – Classic and Sports Car

A mixture of social history and personal insight – Classics Monthly

A funny and informative account of the industry – Autocar

Writing a readable motoring book is difficult enough, but writing something brilliant which gives a totally different outlook on a well covered subject is a true achievement .... it's the warmth of the family story that really makes this book something special – Nick Larkin – Classic Car Weekly

From start to finish it is a thumping good read ... personal, honest and deadly accurate. The notion of using his family as a microcosm for the country at large is very, very clever – Keith Adams – Austin Rover Online

It's informative, well written and extremely funny – anyone who bemoans the demise of the British Car industry should make a beeline for this fantastic book Nat Barnes – Daily Express

ISBN 978-0-9559529-0-6

www.jamesruppert.co.uk
www.foresightpublications.com

The Banger that started it all, a truly awful shed on wheels bought for £80 in 1990. It's a 1978 FSO 125P, which was a collection of sundry Fiat bits and pieces, which were thrown together in the hope that it might just resemble a car. It didn't.

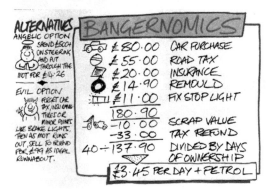

ALTERNATIVES

ANGELIC OPTION

SPEND £500 ON STEERING AND PUT THROUGH THE MOT FOR £4.26

EVIL OPTION

FORGET CAR TAX, INSURANCE TYRES OR MINOR POINTS LIKE BRAKE LIGHTS. THEN AS MOT RUNS OUT, SELL TO FRIEND FOR £99 AS IDEAL RUNABOUT.

BANGERNOMICS

	£80·00	CAR PURCHASE
	£55·00	ROAD TAX
	£20·00	INSURANCE
	£14·90	REMOULD
	£11·00	FIX STOP LIGHT
	180·90	
	−10·00	SCRAP VALUE
	−33·00	TAX REFUND
40÷	137·90	DIVIDED BY DAYS OF OWNERSHIP
	£3·45 PER DAY + PETROL	

Note the sticking plasters holding on the indicator light, grime stained fluffy seat covers and an almost comprehensive tool kit. Plus catch the first ever use of the word Bangernomics in a great magazine called Buying Cars, explaining how running an old Banger can actually make some sort of financial sense.

1

Beginning with a Bang

A sort of introduction, plus Free Bangernomics Support . . . Forever*

A NY IDIOT CAN BUY a used car and every year many do. Also any idiot can run a used car into the ground, but that wouldn't be very clever at all. Often the most idiotic thing that anyone can do is buy a brand-new car and then sell it a few years later at a crippling loss. But even more stupid would be not to learn from that experience, then go back into the showroom and start the whole depreciation process all over again. Yet millions do and for many it doesn't have to be like that.

So welcome to the Bangernomics Bible which explains in the most straightforward terms, how to buy and run a car for less. This is the commonsense and slightly old-fashioned approach to motoring. Once upon a time you bought a car to do a job and then ran it until the vehicle outlived its

*And then there is the question of support. I've been doing that for decades with a quill pen, semaphore, typewriters and sometimes just by shouting. That may not be good enough anymore, so as an act of Bangernomic good faith I promise to provide you with lifetime support. Initially it will be my lifetime, however long that turns out to be, although I will try and sort something out in the far-flung future with relatives and creditors. So while emails and the Internet exists you can contact me (for as long I exist anyway) for biased advice through Bangernomics.com.

usefulness, or failed mechanically, rather than making it part of some sort of lifestyle package. What I mean is, there has been a growing trend for car buyers to convince themselves that it is a matter of urgency to replace their car every three years or sometimes less with another new car.

The great news is that Bangernomics allows you to have your car shaped cake and actually drive it. Because if you love cars then you can buy a dull but reliable domestic appliance on wheels for the weekday commute, whilst in the meantime save enough to buy something much more interesting for the weekend. Or of course you could spend what you save on something flippant like food, or the mortgage. Bangernomics will undoubtedly save money for the motorist who just wants to run a car without breaking the bank and does not give a stuff about acceleration and top speed stats, colour, or anything else that is utterly irrelevant to them.

I wrote Bangernomics back in 1992 when airbags were just bags with air in them, people carriers were still vans with windows and air conditioning meant opening the windows. That has all changed as have the values of used cars and what counts as a Banger. Back in '92 even a reasonable amount of money would only get you a scruffy, possibly unreliable, borderline roadworthy vehicle. Now even a modest budget gives you the pick of a wide variety of vehicles that are often in decent condition with full service histories. The new car culture has changed so much over the last decade that a Banger can now be a car that is just out of manufacturer's warranty. That's because easy and cheap new car finance, the steady reduction in new car retail prices and changing regulations regarding the sales of cars have all helped to bring about a fall in second hand values around the world. Now, even a five to seven year old car can be unwanted and almost worthless, which is why

Bangernomics, as a method of buying and running cars, is still so relevant.

Originally Bangernomics was all about motoring at the blunt end and in many ways it still is, but some of the rules and risks have changed. Put simply, running a cheap and cheaply bought car makes a lot of common and financial sense. Plenty seem to agree with me, setting up websites to celebrate Bangernomics and still ordering copies of the original book. Those copies have long since run out, so the time was well overdue to update Bangernomics.

The principles of buying a used car are simple enough, which is where Bangernomics comes in. I believe we can all make a common sense assessment of an older vehicle without any mechanical knowledge at all. That's why I have decided to strip out most of the technicalities, as there is no point droning on about complicated mechanical failure, when simply stating the obvious would be better. So if something is noisy it's probably broken or about to become even more broken.

Changes from previous Bangernomics editions mean that I have deleted any facts and information which will inevitably date. You can look up a lot of detailed information about specific cars, road taxes and all that on the world wide interweb, which will still exist in some form or other and may well be hard wired into our brains by 2075. So when your grandchildren buy a potato powered hover plane sometime in the future, the same basic principles will apply. I believe that you will only ever need one book on how to buy a personal transportation device (PTD – as they probably won't be called) and the Bangernomics Bible is it.

Indeed the Bangernomics Bible is now truly international as the principles of buying a car and running it for not very much are practised everywhere. Take Cuba, the residents of that country had no alternative but to practise an extreme form of keeping old Bangers running in perpetuity, or at least in Havana. Their resourcefulness is a fantastic example to us all and they may not need the Bangernomics Bible, but anyone planning to buy a car anywhere else in the world might change their motoring habits after reading it. So there will not be any obscure references to the UK car tax system well not that many, or the annual road-worthiness check called the MOT. I will keep the information general and straight-forward in the interests of international understanding and co-operation, but also so that I don't have to rewrite it again.

The Bangernomics Bible is a book which doesn't need much in the way of pictures, which will inevitably date, but they do break up the monotony of a wall of words sometimes. Also I really liked some of the pictures and diagrams from the original book, which are mildly diverting, plus I found a few that had been overlooked and were worth including. I've also revived some ancient cartoons and even brought Slog the Bangernomic Dog out of his kennel after a very long retirement. Not sure if that is a good thing, but potentially Slog the Musical could still happen.

Also what we want to encourage with the Bangernomics Bible is to get people actually looking at cars in the metal again. You might see some pictures on a screen, maybe even a film, but there is never any substitute for actually seeing and driving the car. There is also nothing better than actually meeting the person selling the car. If you don't trust or like them, how can you ever trust the car?

Like the very first edition of Bangernomics you can earn yourself a Bangernomics proficiency certificate if you complete the whole 'crash course' course and buy a car you are really happy with. Send us a picture at Bangernomics.com of you, this book and your Banger and we will send a certificate. How generous is that?

Don't forget that at all times throughout this course you are in safe, if slightly shaky hands. Because when it comes to buying cars I have made every possible mistake. I hope you can learn from them.

So Don't Buy a Dog, buy the Bangernomics Bible. Oh you already have, thanks.

James Ruppert 2009

Free Lifetime Support*: contact the experts at Bangernomics.com for free advice forever on what to buy and where to buy it.

Dedication: To my Father who always took me with him to buy cars and taught me so much and my beautiful Mother who tolerated a boy who filled her house with car and motorcycle parts without ever telling him off.

Thanks: Dee and Olivia for continued support. Steve Cropley for bravely publishing Buying Cars. Matthew Tumbridge at Used Car Expert for understanding what I'm on about.

Illustrations including the front and rear cover by James Ruppert.

All vehicles pictured have inevitably been scrapped by now, however I do rather hope that the Mark 2 Golf GTI has been saved or at least reconstituted into something that is just as much fun.

Publisher's Note: Whilst the Publisher and Author have made every effort to ensure the accuracy of the information contained within this book, no liability can be accepted for any car purchase made. In the case of any

---

*Subject to Terms and Conditions which are lightly touched on in the introduction. Just go to Bangernomics.com to check the latest information and how to claim your certificate.

doubt regarding the condition or safety of the proposed purchase, readers should seek professional advice and not proceed with any purchase where doubt remains. When in doubt get a professional involved because we can't always be there to hold your hand.

2

The Big Bang Theory

Bangernomics Explained

DO YOU WANT TO cut motoring costs? Do you want to buy a good used car? Answer yes to either of those questions and it is a certainty that you need a course in Bangernomics. Just in case you haven't got the message yet, Bangernomics contrasts the absurd expense of buying new, with the supreme good sense of buying used. Bangernomics will de-mystify the art of buying a used car, help you save money and promote safe motoring; it's as simple as that. The worldwide used car market is massive, far more used cars are sold than new, so it is in every motorist's interest to be completely clued up about the Bangernomic lifestyle. However, if you still have lingering doubts, let's deal with some of the most common Bangernomic FAQs (Frequently Asked Questions) as theoretically posed by you. You are represented for no apparent reason as a number of historically significant figures, and a monkey.

How does Bangernomics Save Money?

In both the short and long term a Bangernomic approach to car ownership makes sound financial sense. The truth is that purchasing a new car involves immediate financial losses. Before it has turned a wheel the government imposes all sorts of taxes and that accounts for a large proportion of the purchase price, which has to be written off. Add to that

the dealer's charge to put the car on the road and you can start to feel rather unwell, but the bad news does not end there. Depreciation takes an unhealthy bite out of the car's value too. Depreciation is at its worst in the first year, but it also keeps on eating away during the warranty period and doesn't stop there. With a Banger, or at least a slightly older car all the previous owners have taken the brunt of depreciation and high initial running costs. That leaves the clever Banger buyer with a vehicle that is unlikely to drop in value by very much, having reached rock bottom, or at least close to it. A few years down the line a Banger owner may even get a significant amount of their money back.

But aren't Bangernomic costs the same as a new car?

No. Let's take servicing. Some older cars can be simpler to work on and therefore cheaper to maintain, especially if you carry out some basic checks and repairs yourself. Even if you do buy a fairly complicated and more modern car there are specialists around who can look after it but at much more friendly labour rates. There are also some excellent independent local garages which can often solve problems, rather than simply fit another costly part as main dealers sometimes do. There are also alternative sources for parts rather than paying high main dealer prices. Bangernomics will even show the mechanically cack-handed how to do the minimum maintenance for maximum mileage. In some cases a Bangernomic vehicle only merits the lowest insurance cover. Depending on the age and type of Banger a dent might even improve its looks so an expensive visit to the body shop is unnecessary. Owning an older car means that there is also little reason to worry about the bump and grind of close quarter city traffic and no lost sleep that a vandal might add another scratch to the already weathered paintwork. Of course you should be conscientious about servicing, maintenance and general cosmetics, but you should never be obsessed or worried about getting very minor damage fixed. So Bangernomics helps you take a little bit of stress out of owning and driving a car.

What is a Banger?

Difficult one that. To some people a car becomes a Banger once the ashtrays are full, others may think that it has to be at least a decade old, or when it gets its first stone chip. However, to the student of Bangernomics, it is a car that is attractively cheap, which still has some mileage left in it. Ideally it will be a car that you can afford, rather than one which requires a big loan to

buy. Bangernomic cars are mostly out of manufacturer's warranty and might even have the sort of mileage (100,000 miles plus) that puts some buyers off. As I said in the introduction, things have changed and just about any car that is outside of the manufacturer's warranty can now potentially be classed as a Banger.

Who won't be suited to Bangernomics?

Anyone who spends too much time washing and polishing their car. Snobs who feel obliged keep up with the Motoring Joneses, and must have the latest, most expensive model and then constantly remind everyone how much they paid for it. Basically anyone with more money than sense won't be Bangernomically inclined.

Who benefits from Bangernomics?

Everyone who currently owns a car, or needs to buy one can immediately feel the positive effects of Bangernomics where it matters most, in the pocket. Of course, lower motoring costs are the goal of all private owners who do not have the safety net of a company car. However, even those who have a relatively new model as first-string transport would do well to think about having a usable second car for shopping, or commuting. Why buy a brand new car simply to drive a few miles to the train station?

Is Bangernomics Green?

For you environmentally concerned little greenies out there, it is and it isn't. When you consider the amount of pollution that engines cause, car ownership of any kind could be viewed as irresponsible by extreme car haters. However, a Bangernomic approach means that a car is effectively recycled,  rather than abandoned. The natural resources and energy used to make a new car is phenomenal, which makes prolonging the useful life of a car and then disposing of it responsibly decidedly 'green'. So put your bike in the shed and get motoring.

Is Bangernomics Risky?

Of course it is. Buying a used car brings with it some extra risks, but as Bangernomics shows it is possible, by just using common sense and no specialist technical knowledge, to avoid the worst pitfalls. Indeed, purchasing a new car does not necessarily mean hassle free motoring. It

may break down or prove to be unreliable leaving the buyer with precious few legal remedies. Bangernomics is all about reducing the risk and putting a satisfied smile on your face.

The Bangernomics Bottom Line

If you can afford a brand new car and that's what you want then fine. Just don't start crying when you sell it after a few years and find that it is worth buttons. However, keep it for a decade or two and get full value from it and no one, least of all a Bangernomicist, can argue with you. In previous editions of this book I have compared and contrasted different old, new and slightly old vehicles, but that's something I'd prefer you to do. You will learn a huge amount, especially once you have decided on the type of car and particular model that you think you want. So look at new prices, used values, servicing costs, depreciation and do the arithmetic.

Big Bang Theory – Coursework

Frighten Yourself: Contact some car dealers and ask them how much their new cars cost. However, be on guard and don't get tempted to buy new and slap down a deposit, or you will fail the Bangernomics course at the first stage. That would be a disaster. If what the salesman says does not scare you, do your own bottom line calculations for a basket of similar cars and write down what they cost new, the servicing costs and their value after three years.

Dream on: What would you really like to do or buy? A holiday, a self-improving course in flower arranging or Karate, maybe a set of golf clubs, or a kitchen extension? Get quotes for all those things that could genuinely enhance your life. Many of those things are probably a lot less than the three-year depreciation figure for a brand new car.

Look Forward: Excited at the prospect of buying a cheaper car? So after all that theory let's get down to some real practice and turn to Chapter 3, Bangers & Cash.

3

Bangers & Cash

Budgeting for a Banger

THIS IS SERIOUS. No silly drawings or cartoons as this is a vitally important chapter. Get this wrong and you will be in financial trouble and that means missing the whole point of Bangernomics as a guide for your motoring life.

The true Bangernomics student tips up their piggy bank and shakes out the remaining silver and copper coins to find out what their used car budget really is. If you don't know how much you can afford it will certainly all end in tears. In the long term borrowing money ends up costing you money because of interest charges. Yes there are people who don't realise that, or just don't care. That means you must carry out some basic budgeting, not only to arrive at a sum which goes towards the purchase, but also a weekly allowance that proves you can afford to run the car. This is basic housekeeping and if you have never sat down and worked out what you can afford, now is the time to start. And so you can't wriggle out of your budgeting commitments I want you to write the figures in this book in ink. Don't even think about changing that figure unless you suddenly come into a lot of money courtesy of a great new job, lottery win or an inheritance.

GET BUDGETING: The logic is simple, how much do you want to spend? £_____ (write it down). How much do you have saved? £_____ (write it down). If there is a shortfall, then think again. If there is a surplus, is that enough to constitute 'savings' given your lifestyle and requirements? If you can't afford it, then maybe you should forget about buying for a few months. The Bangernomics approach is to do a bit of overtime, save up and use your own hard-earned cash to qualify for the Bangernomics course. If nothing else, it concentrates your mind wonderfully on making a purchase that you won't regret. Even if you make a mistake and buy a dud then at least you won't be paying for it over the next 12, 24 or 36 months or more as you would with a loan. Once you have decided to spend a certain amount on the car write it down in this book in ink. As you will know or soon discover, the big problem when buying a car is that you can get carried away and end up spending more than you have budgeted for. It could be a persuasive salesman, or your own weakness when your heart overrules your head and authorises a costly impulse buy.

YOUR BUYING BUDGET: So the simple question is: how much can you actually afford? That figure is your budget. You really ought to know how to arrive at this figure, but just in case you can't cope: add up all your weekly/monthly outgoings and expenditures and set that against your income.

INCOME £_____(Salary/Wage/Bank Interest)

LESS EXPENDITURE £_____
   (Mortgage/Rent/Local Taxes/Electricity etc)

TOTAL £_____

Again put these figures in ink and stick to them. Obvious really. What's left is how much you have to cover insurance, any road taxes, insurance, fuel costs and maintenance of your next car. Is it enough? Do you have savings? Are you prepared to spend all or some of those on buying the car? Lots of questions but they do have to be answered.

SO MY BUYING BUDGET IS £_____ (in ink please). If you have not got the savings then . . .

BORROWING: There used a be a few pages on how to borrow and I've junked that now. It's never good to borrow and I think you should avoid it at all costs. At best get a loan from a family member who is going to be lenient and hopefully won't break your legs if you fall behind with repayments. Also an employer might give a soft loan to guarantee that you actually turn up for work. Otherwise just save up.

Bangers & Cash Coursework

Calculate to accumulate

If you haven't already done it, get a big bit of paper and properly work out exactly what your incomings and outgoings really are. You might do this each week anyway, but many don't. It is depressing, but essential especially as motoring is so expensive these days and takes a huge chunk of your household budget.

4

Head Bangers

Before you Buy

BANGERNOMICS IS NOT JUST about choosing a used car because it is cheap. Bangernomics can only be practised successfully if the student is prepared to consider all the options and think everything through. Preparation is the key to a stress free Bangernomics inspired purchase.

WHICH CAR?: You would think that deciding what type of car you want would be easy. Not so. Lots of people leave their house having decided on a three-door hatchback, only to return from the showroom a few hours later in a stretch limousine. Salesmen can be very persuasive and it is all too easy to fall in love with an inappropriate and impractical car when buying from a car dealer or privately.

SIZE MATTERS: Will it fit? How big is your drive, garage, car port, or even parking space outside your house, or place of work? There is no point buying a car that is going to be too big. Sounds obvious, but you should take measurements.

Will they fit? Don't forget that it isn't just you who will be using the car. Dogs, children and spouses/partners must be able to fit in. Also, are you sitting comfortably? Bad back, tall, short, fat, thin, we are all different shapes, sizes and have different ailments. If you want to avoid the osteopath's table make sure the driver's seat is supportive and that the steering column adjusts and that you can see out clearly.

Can it cope? What do you want your next car to do? Tow a caravan? Then it needs a large engine and maybe four-wheel drive. Local journeys? Then a small hatchback will do. Got a lifestyle and hobbies to follow up at the weekend? Maybe an estate would be good. Only you know. There is nothing worse than having the wrong car for the job. An offroader just for the urban school run could be daft, so is a cramped coupé for a family of four. **Sum Up:** Get the basics straight before you buy.

WHICH ENGINE?

We can have a great big debate about what sort of engine to choose. Petrol, diesel, hybrid, LPG (Liquid Petroleum Gas), battery, who knows? The secret is getting the engine that suits you. It may be purely about what you can afford, what is available and the driving conditions. If you only cover a small mileage then an ultra efficient engine may not be the answer. By contrast a big inefficient unit that doesn't do that many miles to the gallon may be fine. Ask friends and relatives what they think is the easiest to live with. Get all that opinion especially when it comes to running costs and reliability and make a decision based on the real world, then apply it to what you want to do.

IMAGE IS EVERYTHING AND NOTHING

Even though many would like to think we'd only buy a car for sensible, practical and financial reasons, actually what the car looks like, and says about us is often a vitally important part of the decision making process. It is all about credibility and some cars have it, whilst others don't. A strong image means a car will hold its value well and be easier to resell. A low image makes it much more affordable. It is important to remember that often image has nothing to do with reliability, or ability. The choice is yours.

Sum Up: Bangernomics students don't care about image, only the practicality of the car and its affordability.

EXTRA EXTRA

What a used car comes fitted with is extremely important, however it won't necessarily make it worth more, but it will be easier to live with and may eventually be less bother to resell. The significance for students of Bangernomics is that a lack of certain features can seriously down value a car and make it more difficult to sell, that's great news for those of us on the Bangernomics course that want value.

Good Extras: Safety sells so ABS brakes and airbags are always in demand and many Bangernomics students may regard these items as essential. Cars without them, especially older ones are cheap. Luxury and executive cars must have leather trim and automatic gearboxes so if they don't have them that's another reason why you will pay less. Small cars don't need much, although in the non-Bangernomic buying world power steering is essential now and increasingly air conditioning is becoming a must have to help a car sell at a strong price. If you can live without luxuries, or ones that don't work, then you can save a lot of money.

Bad Extras: Certainly don't pay more for an expensive music system, alloy wheels, or anything else which could be regarded as 'cheering up' an otherwise ordinary car like for instance body kit and spoilers. If someone other than the manufacturer has fitted engine immobilisers and alarms, they often can go wrong, or just go off randomly. Yes DIY add ons are bad. Also, special edition models are usually not worth more than the standard car so don't be misled into paying more.

Colour Matters, or rather it doesn't to the Bangernomics student. Anything dull such as brown, or dark ('doom') blue is regarded as bad by the car trade. Flat colours must be strong to survive in the used car marketplace. Metallic colours are reckoned to be the best, but again they must be strong. Briefly fashionable colours, usually bright ones have a habit of going out of fashion, so choose carefully, or pay a lot less. If you can live with a dodgy paint finish or you are colour blind, bring on the badly painted car. Unless you plan on reselling the car fairly quickly it pays not to be bothered. If the cosmetics on a car are poor that is another reason to pay less. Provided the car hasn't been seriously damaged, (and you will find out how to spot this later) poor paint or a scruffy car should not be an obstacle to getting a better value Banger.

The golden rule is buy the best-equipped car you can afford, but never pay extra, for extras. Be prepared to own and live with a weird colour and the wrong sorts of extras, or even extras that don't work if it means that you will get a better value Banger.

WHEN TO BUY: The used car market operates all year round, meaning that good cars will always sell, whatever the weather. Sometimes the availability and prices of used cars can change on a seasonal basis. So as well as having your wits, facts and figures about you, don't forget to consult the calendar and look out of the window at what's going on. The fortunes of the new and used car markets have traditionally been linked to a change of model or registration year. So when that happens this creates an artificially high demand for new cars and to help pay for them, a larger number of part exchanges flood into the car trade. This situation provides a variety of opportunities for the Banger buyer after a bargain.

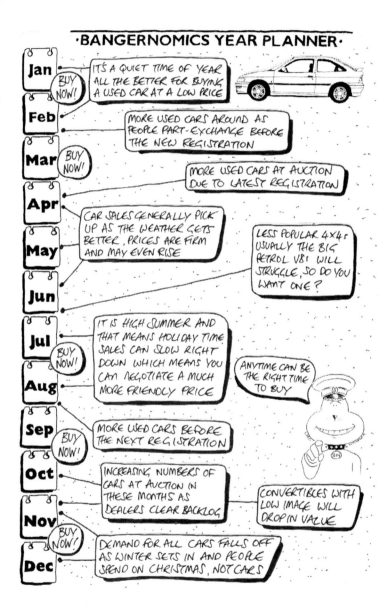

So increased used car activity starts leading up to a plate/year change as the rate of part-exchanges starts to rise quite noticeably and that means more bargains for used car buyers. More used cars means lower prices. Auctions become noticeably busier as the part-exchanges that didn't move off the forecourt are given their last chance. So if you're confident enough to buy at Auction (see Bangers Under the Hammer) it's likely that you can pick up a freshly cleaned and prepared car at a very good price.

Weather conditions can also have an effect. In the winter many can't be bothered to go out in the cold and look for a car unless they have to. Then, as soon as the days get longer and spring officially, rather than actually, arrives, every-one's thoughts turn to forming a new relationship with a car. Obviously a mild winter can buoy up a usually lacklustre used car market, whilst a long hot summer gets everyone excited about motoring and sales reach record levels along with the temperature. But then again summer holidays when people go away can cause certain models to sell particularly badly depending on the time of year. There is a logicality about it all, so a convertible reaches a low point just before Christmas (or when it's very cold) and a 4x4 isn't a high priority during the spring and summer months. However, all it takes is a washout summer to send prices and demand down. If you can anticipate and take advantage of the seasonal swings and roundabouts, good. If you need a car tomorrow, don't worry too much about the weather and just get on with it. The Bangernomics Year Planner is a bit of a distraction, but it is a pretty accurate reflection of what happens subject to registration plate and model year changes in your part of the world.

WHICH BANGER? There are thousands of Bangers for sale at any one time and the choice can be bewildering. The best approach is to draw up a shortlist of no more than four or five specific models that you think fit your requirements. As a result, you will not be distracted by other cars that might be a similar price, but are unsuitable. You may already have your own set of preferences and prejudices, but there are a few simple guidelines, which should keep you out of trouble.

PRIZE BANGER There is no photofit for what makes the perfect banger, but if you do want to contain running costs and reduce your chances of breaking down there are some types of car you should be aiming for.

Mainstream Model: Go for a well-known make and a mainstream popular model. Every garage can cope with a service and parts availability ought to be excellent and cheap. Insurance won't be an issue either, with low insurance ratings and an affordable premium on well-known models.

Basic Specification: It is getting difficult to avoid electric windows and roofs and even air conditioning, but if you do want the minimum maintenance, hassle and expense when things go wrong it has to be the basic or poverty model. Trouble is, that will reduce your comfort levels, but then if you are simply using this Banger for a local commute you don't want anything too complicated or clever as that will cost a fortune to put right.

Engine: You definitely want one of those, it is just a case of what form it will take in the future, plus what you find underneath the bonnet depends on how you want to approach Bangernomic motoring and maintenance. If you need a high performance model or a luxury car then the bigger engine comes pretty much as standard. Ideally the engine should be appropriate for the model and how you intend to use it. However, bigger multi-cylinder petrol engines are always cheaper for the simple reason that they deliver fewer miles to the gallon. If you only cover a small mileage that might be a

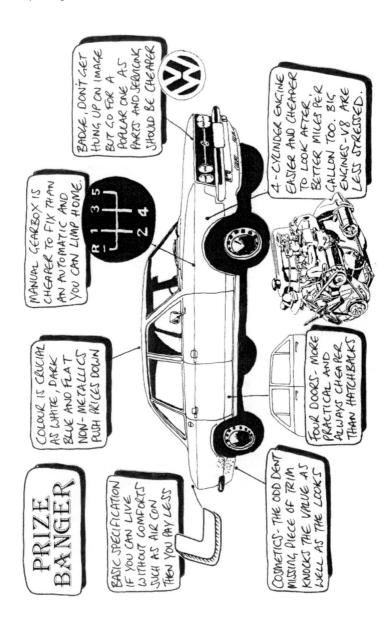

sacrifice worth making. Big engines are less stressed and as a result can be bought with larger mileages.

Manual Gearbox: If you prefer an automatic, or only have an automatic driving licence, then there is no contest, but when they go wrong it will usually cost double the amount for a manual gearbox. A manual is also slightly more flexible, more fuel-efficient and in an emergency able to limp home on just a few operational gears.

Four Doors: Not compulsory, and indeed not an option on a coupé, but it means more flexibility and practicality for the family and business car user. Hatchbacks and estates are not only easy to live with, but can be easier to resell in some locations. However, saloons are very popular in some world markets, so the more doors the better.

WHICH FLAVOUR BANGER? (with some pictures just in case you forgot what they sort of looked like).

TOWN CENTRE TOTS – CITY CARS
I'm assuming that what you want is a town centre assault vehicle and not much more. Something for local journeys and not the annual 35K mile slog up and down the motor-way. What you really want here is, cheap and cheerful and above all, small.

Prices: Firm as they are in high demand, especially when sold in built-up areas.

Verdict: Don't buy if you travel long distances.

HAPPY SHOPPERS – SMALL HATCHBACKS

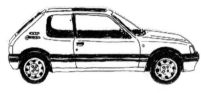

Some people call them superminis, but essentially these are the second car and shopping hatches that dominate the market place especially in European and far eastern countries. They can be bought privately and be well looked after, when the mileage stays low and the service book full. However, once they have had multiple owners their condition can deteriorate rapidly as servicing becomes optional for some careless owners. Companies use them as pool cars sometimes and that also means that they can be in poor cosmetic condition when sold.

Prices: Can be rather high especially in built up areas where more people want conveniently small shopping trolleys. Automatics are particularly sought after.

Verdict: Demand for good examples outstrips supply and mostly you will get what you pay for because there are always tatty ones on sale.

FAMILY FUNMOBILES

These are the saloons or hatches that are basically company cars. So-called executive cars are mixed up with this lot too, posh ones with upmarket badges in some cases and lots of extras that we can buy at some very low prices. When bought by a private owner and looked after they make a great buy. Many are also bought commercially and provided you buy examples with few previous owners they still have lots of life left in them. Beware, the body might look straight, but the mechanicals could be on their last legs. Interior condition could be ragged if it has been used as a surrogate van.

Prices: Generally low as the large numbers around means buyers are spoilt for choice.

Verdict: Good all round ability, but avoid over tired examples.

A BIT OF ESTATE These can come in small, medium and large sizes. Mostly bought to do a job and that can mean that they have led a hard life. So whether it is coping with an extended family and their hobbies or a business user with business to do, the estate can sometimes be in marginal condition. When they deputise for builders' vans, the interior can be shot. Same goes for the suspension, which can take a lot of punishment.

Prices: Estates can be worth more than hatchbacks and certain models are considerably more desirable than the saloons.

Verdict: Requires careful selection and must be bought on condition rather than price.

LUXOBARGE Can a luxury car ever be called a banger? Well, why not? What you get is an awful lot of car for hardly any money. For some just running a car like this for a few years is fun. Also when some pointless electrical system breaks (e.g. heated seats) there is no point in fixing it. Also big cars have big unstressed engines and components that should last longer. Our old friend depreciation also means that prices are on the floor pretty much permanently. The downside is always going to be high running costs in terms of fuel and when things go wrong. The increasing technology is a pain and can make simple diagnosis of problem an expensive undertaking. Obviously if anything breaks they can cost a lot to fix, but that's why salvage/scrap/spare parts yards were invented. You should be able to get second-hand parts at affordable prices and of course you would never go near a main agent for servicing would you?

Prices: Can be very cheap as few buyers really want complicated old cars that are potentially expensive to run.

Verdict: A well looked after example could last you a good few years. Not for everyone, but you can be very smug indeed about how little it cost to buy.

PAUPER PERFORMERS Why not? Banger buyers can have fun too getting some style on the cheap. These days a lot of models can qualify as a performance car and the vast majority are bought by enthusiasts. However, the time to avoid them is when they slip into the hands of those who can't afford to run them. That is because proper servicing and insurance is always going to be higher than for standard models.

Prices: Performance cars with an image are more costly, but depreciation on the majority of models is quite heavy which makes them bargains, especially after they go out of manufacturer warranty.

Verdict: Expensive to own from maintenance to insurance, but depreciation means some real bargains.

LOFTY ROADERS Which are a bit daft if you are trying to save money but if bought to do a job can be worthwhile. Petrol engines are the death for values in Europe. They can have lots  of equipment and are over engineered to the point where they could last you a lifetime especially as so few ever go off road. There are several types of four-wheel drive vehicles from so-called lifestyle off roaders, which are smaller, and the heavy-duty 4x4s designed for farmers. Many are bought for style and image rather than ability. However, some can lead harder lives. Ideally you should have a purpose in mind for a 4x4, such as towing or real off roading because running costs are more expensive than for a conventional car. Not only that, 4x4s are slower, less comfortable and don't handle like a car, hence the popularity of the smaller lifestyle models.

Prices: For the larger petrol engine models prices fall dramatically. Diesels fare better and the small lifestyle models are the most sought after and have firm values.

Verdict: Only appropriate for the Bangernomics student who is going to make some use of the car's capabilities. Otherwise the higher maintenance costs and petrol consumption could be big penalties.

BANGER BUSES People Carriers or MPVs (multi purpose vehicles), once derided as vans with windows, are now actually high-rise estate cars. You can mostly get six or seven on board in comfort, but the drawback is there isn't room for much luggage. Being a multi purpose vehicle though means that the seats can be moved around, or taken out completely to offer more flexibility. Mostly family owned, but also bought commercially by amongst others, taxi companies. Often people carriers can be in well-used condition so buyers have to be careful.

Prices: The sheer number around and the realisation by some owners that they don't need all that space means that particularly petrol models (rather than diesel) are good value.

Verdict: If you need the space then the People Carrier is perfect, but be aware of its limitations.

MINI BUSES Essentially a high rise hatchback and often called compact people carriers by cleverly repackaging the interior so there is more flexible space. However, many of these models only seat the standard five bodies, but at least have room for some luggage. Like any other vehicle they can lead hard lives and look scruffy, or on the other hand be well cared for.

Prices: Although there are increasing numbers on the used market, demand is high for the right, well-equipped models and prices can be firm.

Verdict: Makes sense as family transport, but maybe a cheaper conventional estate or hatchback would do with a low Bangernomic price tag.

CLASSIC BANGERS Just a few words about what is a very special case. The decision to buy an older or classic car is usually an emotional, rather than practical one, but that  doesn't mean you should buy the first classic you fall in love with. The condition of a classic can vary hugely as it may have had one careful enthusiast owner, or be a multi-owner patched-up rust bucket. You don't want to buy a liability because the whole point of choosing a classic as an everyday car is that it will be easy to own and only certain models are. You have to go for mainstream classics where parts availability is good and there is a nationwide network of specialists and owners' clubs. For light local use a classic offers cheaper parts, less things to go wrong, the possibility of straightforward DIY maintenance and minimal depreciation and even possible appreciation. However, before you even consider buying you must find out everything you can about the classic you want, or think you want. So read books and classic car magazines for guidance, study prices and talk to specialists. **Drive** the classic (borrow or hire) to find out if you really could live with your dream classic. **Join** the relevant owners' club, which gives access to unrivalled expert knowledge about the classic and often the best examples for sale. **Never buy** a restoration project. It may start out cheap, but it will prove expensive longer term and you may never finish it. **Always** get an expert to check the classic, that way you won't buy a dud, or pay over the odds.

Prices: There is no need to pay a fortune, classic cars can be great value and if maintained properly won't depreciate very much. However, some owners are less realistic and more attached to their cars than others.

Verdict: The Bangernomics student investigates every possibility and the practical classic may make sense for you. Just don't buy a costly liability.

WHITE VAN MAN Bought by companies and sometimes driven by psychopaths. Abuse multiplies down the chain of ownership until it looks and drives like a shed. If bought direct from a company with a full history it may make sense, but more often Mr Local Builder is unloading a rusty, mechanically worn-out heap. Rear load areas and doors often rusty and damaged, suspension and the engine may also need attention.

Prices: Can seem attractively low but as this may be classed as a commercial vehicle, beware the extra tax which needs to be paid in some cases, especially if you are buying from a company.

Verdict: Often run into the ground before sale so be careful. Just the two seats. Criminals like breaking in to see if there are any tools/valuables in the back. Not for everyone then.

You should now be able to put together your short or wish list ...

BANGER SHORTLIST

1._____
2._____
3._____
4._____
5._____

BANGER VALUES Now find out if you can afford any of the cars on your banger shortlist. It is simply a case of looking through car adverts and jotting down prices of the cars you like the sound of. Ideally check out cars local to you as this will give you a feel for the market. Also if you want to buy a cheap car there is no point wandering too far for a Banger so try and keep your search within reasonable travelling distance.

If possible, understand why one car is priced higher than another, find out whether it has had one owner or thirty two, has a valid roadworthiness certificate, whether it is a private, or dealer sale, all these things make a difference.

Price guides are just that, guides either in magazine or online form. The condition of the car itself and the deal you can negotiate is always the deciding factor. Also, some price guides may only cover cars up to a certain age, so it may not include the Banger you had mind. However, you should now be able to put an average price on your short/wish list.

BANGER SHORTLIST (compile your shortlist with rough price guide)

1._____ £_____

2._____ £_____

3._____ £_____

4._____ £_____

5._____ £_____

6._____ £_____

INSURANCE

So you have sort of decided what model and maybe what make of car you'd like to buy. How about insurance then? Sorting it out now is the sensible thing to do because it could help you change your mind about the sort of Banger you intend to look for. It is pointless buying a car and then finding that it is in a high insurance group and you can't afford it. Shopping for insurance is easy, you just have to invest a bit of time. Ideally get plenty of quotes. So here is the briefest guide to car insurance, which uses the UK system as basis, but the same basic principles apply worldwide.

Decide on the cover you want. In the UK there is Third Party Fire & Theft which covers the damage you do to someone else and their property, also allowing for the car to be stolen, or set alight. This is worth considering for an old and very cheap car. Then there is Comprehensive which pays for most of the damage resulting from an accident, much better for a more valuable car and for peace of mind as hire car charges and tow in fees may be included.

Factors affecting insurance: 1. *The Car.* Ease of repair, cost of repair, performance, cost when new. Also any modifications may affect the amount the policy costs, such as tuning the engine, or fitting alloy wheels. Installing extra security measures though should help reduce the premium paid. **2.** *Your Home.* If you live in a town or city there are higher chances of theft, or an accident. Garaging a car often helps reduce the premium. **3.** *Use.* Lots of named drivers raises the premium's price, also if the car is primarily used for business rather than private journeys that can increase what you pay. **4.** *You.* You could be a bad risk because of your driving record. Usually anyone under 25 years old automatically pays a higher premium. Over 50? Good news, you are less of a risk and should pay less.

Policy Details. Excess is a voluntary and also compulsory amount that you will pay an agreed sum in the event of a claim. The higher the excess, the lower the premium. **No Claims Discount.** So building up a claims free driving record means the cost of the policy will be reduced each year until the discount reaches 60%. This bonus can also be protected for an extra amount, in the event of making a claim. **Special Policies.** These are available for certain kinds of drivers in particular professions (i.e. from hairdressers, to nurses), or those over a certain age (mature drivers). Under this category also comes classic car policies (mostly for cars over 15 years old), where account is taken of how cherished the car is and that the mileage is likely to be restricted annually (say 5,000 or less).

Sum Up. Get at least ten quotes based on exactly the same requirements and then compare the cover and additional benefits on offer which may include free windscreen replacement, or even membership of a rescue organisation. Getting quotes online or by some remote device has never been easier. Now write down the best quote you have.

INSURANCE QUOTE £_____ COMPANY_____
Notes

OVERALL CAR EXPENSES – WEEKLY/MONTHLY

Now let's see if you can afford the car. Try these calculations out on your Banger shortlist and see if there is a noticeable cost difference.

INSURANCE: simply divide the quote by 12 or 52 for the weekly or monthly figure.

PETROL: Estimate how many miles you will drive each year (the national average is reckoned to be 12,000 in the UK, but if you are only going to do local trips then it could be much lower, say 3-6,000). Then research the average fuel consumption figure for your Banger. Divide that figure by the mileage, then multiply that by whatever the horrendous cost of petrol may be £_____ to arrive at a figure £_____ that you can then divide by 12 or 52 to arrive at the weekly or monthly figure.

ROAD TAX: Depending on where you are, there may be a charge for keeping a car or renewing the registration/number plate. In the UK it is far too complicated to mention any specific rules or guidance suffice to say that you should research just what the car you think you want will cost, usually based on engine size and type, age, emissions and probably how many cuddly toys you can get in the boot.

SERVICING: Whether or not you plan on tackling the servicing yourself telephone a local garage for quotes about routine maintenance and a major service (usually expensive garage visits happen at certain set mileages) and then allow an extra sum on top for interim repairs and replacements, such as an exhaust, brakes or tyres. It is vital to find out what sundry items like this cost. If the basic parts cost a fortune then could you really afford to run it?

Basic Service	£_____
Major Service	£_____
Tyre	£_____
Brake Pads	£_____

DEPRECIATION: A tricky question as no one (despite what they claim) can really predict what a car will be worth in a year's time, but looking at the prices being asked for second-hand ones and comparing that to the price when new is the easiest way of doing this. However, when cars get very cheap they may depreciate barely at all, or even be worth the same amount if they are still roadworthy and saleable.

With all those figures to hand you can now put them in a table and see if you can make a decision based purely on what it costs to run.

Car	1	2	3	4	5
Petrol					
Insurance					
Servicing					
Road Tax					
Depreciation					

So now you know whether you can afford the Banger of your dreams. Remember, stick to your budgets and don't be tempted to overspend. Finally, if you are already a car owner and plan to replace it with a Banger, refer to the BYE BYE BANGER chapter for tips on how to dispose of your car. It is in your interests to sell your car first, or at least plan the sale so that the two transactions take place roughly at the same time. You will be in a better position to negotiate with a wad of money in your pocket. If you are buying from a dealer then there is always the possibility of part-exchanging your car. This saves you the hassle of selling, but you will pay a higher price because you won't get the full value for your old car. However in the BANGER BANTER chapter we will tell you how best to tackle a part-exchange deal.

Head Bangers – Coursework

Talk cars

If this chapter has confused or frightened you in any way then maybe you don't know much about cars. Don't worry there's lots of magazines, websites, TV programmes, or whatever media delivery system is preferred at the time you are reading this, which can help you out. Also speak to friends and family who own cars and ask them what they think, everyone has an opinion about cars. Most of them are misguided, mad and just plain wrong, but don't let that stop you listening.

Drive cars

Drive them. Go to car dealers, showrooms, answer adverts, just go and look at, touch and most importantly drive them. Within seconds you can probably tell whether you are happy or not behind the wheel. This is absolutely vital. Also important is talking to everyone who is crucial to the decision making process whether it is your dog, or your children. Do they fit, are they comfortable and most importantly, are they happy?

Think cars

At this stage of Banger buying it is vital to keep your mind wide open. Indeed, you may start to dream Bangers, which isn't a bad thing. What should happen is the right vehicle for you and your family will slowly become obvious.

5

Browsing for Bangers

Finding your Banger

YOU KNOW YOU CAN afford it, insure it and roughly what you want. Now where is it? For the Bangernomics student, they are everywhere. The Interweb has shrunk the car market so that any vehicle can be seen in some detail within seconds. If you are buying a cheaper car, or Banger then the best advice is to keep it local. What's the point in tearing all over the country wasting petrol, travelling costs and time looking at a load of old wrecks when you can do that on your doorstep? More importantly, if you want to bring something to the seller's attention it is better to do it to someone who lives locally and also remind him or her that you are only a bus ride away. Otherwise this is the part of the Bangernomics Bible that could date the fastest, as many of these outlets may no longer exist. There will though always be professionals making a living selling cars who are usually called dealers. Private sellers are unlikely to stop trying to sell their old cars, and most frightening of all criminals, scammers and fraudsters will always try and separate a car buyer from their money. Certainly most car sales have become primarily digital and that is likely to be your first contact with the car and/or seller.

INTERWEB From the comfort of your own computer terminal it is possible to surf the World Wide Web, or in

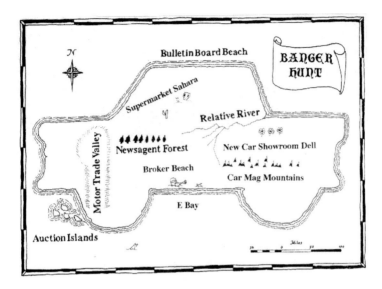

reality – your nationwide web for a used car. So simply sit back and click your mouse as they used to say. There are online editions of classified advertisement magazines offering excellent search facilities, by make, model, post code and budget taking the strain out of reading every page of their paper editions. Not only that, with many ads you can also click to see colour pictures, video films and probably 3D presentations. There are also countless online classified ad sites linked either to magazines, newspapers and owners' clubs and they are just a search engine click away. Not only that, most independent and franchised dealers now have sites so that you can look at their used stock and many manufacturers offer direct links to their dealers who operate official used car schemes.

For: Instantaneous. Mostly up to date.
Against: You can't test drive over the net.

CAR SUPERMARKETS More new cars than the market knew what to do with has resulted into the over spill being stocked at so-called Car Supermarkets where hundreds of cars are on sale. Their philosophy of park them deep and sell them cheap has largely worked, although it is not always possible to haggle a better deal. Also their part exchange offers can be disappointing. Best for nearly new cars, as older stock direct from auctions can look shabby and poor value. As ever the golden rule is, shop around.

For: Huge choice. Some low prices.
Against: Poor part exchange deals, can't haggle.

VIRTUAL CAR SUPERMARKETS As above and you can view lots of cars online, but you don't test drive. You just pay online, the cars are usually inspected and warranted, which is good. However, they don't always want your old car, which can be inconvenient for some. They usually undercut a traditional dealer.

For: Keen prices, easy to buy.
Against: Can't test drive, or haggle.

AUCTIONS Things happen fast at an auction, remember that and you won't go far wrong. If you miss bidding for one car, another one will be along literally in a minute. It pays to be cautious and do plenty of homework. That means several visits without your wallet to see how it all operates. Listening carefully to what the auctioneer says before each lot is vital. A one-owner example with a warranted mileage and full service history is obviously the sort of Banger to bid for. For the less experienced it is easy to get caught out because an auction can be a clearing-house for unwanted part exchanges and 'problem' cars. It is also easy to get carried away and bid too much.

You will not be able to drive the car before sale, although with a warranted car the right of rejection exists for a major fault discovered within a limited period after the sale. There are though individual traders who will buy cars for you at auction. They charge a flat percentage fee and will only buy the model and specification you want. Obviously you can bid in person and increasingly online in real time and actually see the car being driven on your TV/Computer screen.

For: Trade prices, specialist traders who will bid for you.
Against: Very risky. **See Further: Bangers Under the Hammer.**

ONLINE AUCTIONS Like a traditional real life auction but virtual and in many ways even scarier. The best known at the time of writing is Ebay. This is where a seller uploads details and pictures of the car they want to sell and then you are expected to bid on it and actually buy if your bid is the highest. Although if the car is ultimately not as described you should be able to get out of completing the transaction. There is however no substitute for actually going to see and drive it.

For: You may get a car for less. Easy to do.
Against: You may not bother travelling to see the car before you bid. That could cause you problems.

Bangernomic Top Tips for buying online

1. Try to bid on a car in your area that ideally you can test drive.
2. If there is a long, detailed description, listing good and bad points, and lots of photographs, then those are all good signs that you are dealing with a conscientious and hopefully honest seller.

3. So the opposite is true, avoid short adverts with few details, or ads with small and fuzzy pictures. You really can't tell the condition of a car from a thumbnail sized picture.

4. Don't get carried away, you should always check out prices for similar vehicles at dealers and in other adverts to make sure you're not bidding too much.

5. Remember that in the UK at least, if the vehicle doesn't match the description, then the seller has misrepresented it, and you don't have to buy it if you win the auction. However, if you do win, and the advert is accurate, you're legally obliged to complete the transaction.

6. Never pay until you've seen the car is the most obvious piece of advice, but so few people follow it.

7. Check out the seller's feedback on the advert. If they've sold a lot of cars in the past, be cautious. They could be a dealer, or someone behaving like one and shirking their tax paying responsibilities, as there will be minimal legal comeback and no warranty.

NEW CAR SHOWROOMS Yes really. You could trace your chosen Bangers back one stage to the car showroom by approaching the sales manager and asking if they have any part exchange vehicles they want to shift. The advantage to them is that the car is sold more quickly, without paying an auctioneer's commission and they may get a better price from you than from a car trader. For your part of the bargain you need to make a decision quickly, make the payment in cash and undertake to buy 'as seen' with no comebacks. Not for those who lack confidence then. However, if you think you can handle the pressure, contact the sales manager, explain who you are and most importantly the amount you want to spend. If you are not too fussy about the type of car/Banger then you will get a faster and more positive response. If scrap car values are very low it has become possible to buy a part exchanged car for a nominal sum. The dealer does not want the hassle or the expense of paying for an otherwise unsaleable car to go for scrap. Better to sell it to you for a token amount.

For: A used car at a trade price.
Against: You have to act like a professional and make an instant decision.

BROKERS Although strongly associated with the new car market, independent brokers can also source nearly new, ex management and ex dealer demonstrator stock at significant savings. It is worth asking lots of questions, some cars could be those returned under no quibble car warranty schemes and may be faulty. Beware any brokers who ask for a big deposit and establish where the car is coming from before handing over any money.

For: They do the haggling for you.
Against: Some may string you along without having access to the car you really want. Cars on offer are not likely to be Bangers.

FRIENDS & FAMILY There are strong reasons for not buying from your nearest and dearest. What if they sell you a rubbish used car? What if they ask too much? That is the risky element in all Bangernomics transactions. However, you have nothing to lose by putting the word about that you are in the market for a car. They might know someone, who knows someone else's friend's cousin's mate with the perfect car at a knock down price. At least you stand a chance of getting a truthful report on the condition and history of the car. Well possibly.

For: A car at a knock down price because you are a friend/relative.

Against: Blood is thicker than water, so limited come back if there is a problem, which could cause a long-standing family rift.

BULLETIN BOARDS: In staff canteens, near the checkout at supermarkets and DIY superstores, leisure centre foyers and in the newsagent's window – yes those informative little post cards are everywhere. Amongst the three-piece suites and emergency plumbers are countless cars in various states of disrepair. This is a popular outlet for motors at the truly Banger end of the market, always worth a look.

For: Cheap local cars.

Against: Can also be cheap, local, rubbish cars.

MAGAZINES/NEWSPAPERS: These could be yesterday's news by the time you read this, and in many ways the online editions have taken over and many have links to classified car adverts anyway. Also the localised editions of classified ad magazines may have a limited life with limited appeal.

For: Loads of cars mainly nearby.

Against: Just one, or maybe no pictures at all, plus you must act quickly to get the bargains.

CAR MAGAZINES: The problem with most car magazines is that almost all are published on a monthly basis. So if they do have classified ads by the time you get around to enquiring the car has long gone. If, however, you are in the market for a classic car or a particular make you are much better served as there are specialist magazines in these areas.

For: If you are after a particular model of car.
Against: Car may be sold by the time you call.

SMALL AD SHORTHAND: Some car advertisements are at first sight almost impossible to decipher. That is because the seller is saving money by often over-abbreviating the information. New and more obscure abbreviations are invented every day, but these are the essential and most common ones used in classified ads and on the Internet.

A, AW Alloys = alloy wheels
A, Auto = automatic gearbox
ABS = Anti-skid braking system
Air, A/C = air conditioning
Autochanger = multiple CD player
BHP = brake horse power,
output of the engine
CAT = Approved Category alarm
C/L, c/locking = central locking
Climate C/C = fully automatic air conditioning
Cruise = cruise control, maintains a set speed
E/A, E/Aerial = electric aerial
EDM, e/m, edm = electric mirrors, door mirrors
ESR, E/sunroof = electric sunroof
EW, E/windows = electric windows
Fi i, inj, in = fuel injection
FSH FS/RS History = full service history
/some history
HR = head restraints FHR front and RHR rear
HWW = headlamp wash/wipe

K = 000 miles prefixed by a number
LHD = left hand drive
LPT = low profile tyres, thin sports tyres
usually on alloys
LSD = limited slip differential, fitted to sports cars
Ltd Ed = limited edition model
LWB = long wheelbase, longer vehicle
M, Met, MP = metallic paint
MF, M/flaps = mud flaps
MIs/mlg = miles, mileage
MOT = car has an MOT certificate in UK
MPG = miles per gallon
MSR = manual sunroof
O/D = overdrive (5th type gear) fitted to classics
and some four wheel drive
ONO = or near offer, the seller is inviting offers
PAS/PS = power steering
Power (e.g. windows) = electric (windows, roof etc)
POA = price on application, the seller won't reveal the price
PX, part-ex = part exchange accepted
R/C = radio cassette and CD obviously
SH = service history
SR = sunroof
Stacker = multiple CD player
T & T = taxed and tested
T, (T) = trade sale
TG, Tints = tinted glass
VGC = very good condition
W/W = wide wheels
4WD/4x4 = four wheel drive

You vs. Seller Now you are ready to start responding to adverts, but now you need to be good at psychology. You could come across a decent, honest and helpful private seller with a perfect specimen to sell, or meet a rogue with a rough old car. You never can tell. The majority are honest, but some may have bought an awful car without realising it, or maybe they have lost all the service history and possibly their advertisement misdescribes the car. Worst of all they think their car is worth a fortune. So if you thought buying from the motor trade is fraught with danger, a private seller can be even worse. The fact is you have fewer rights if you buy privately. The car must be as described by the seller. If a private seller lies about the condition of the car, you can in most countries take legal action for your losses, providing you can find the seller and want to go to the trouble of pursuing a claim through the courts. Obviously there is a huge amount of difference between a private seller against whom a buyer has virtually no redress and full time dealer who usually has all sorts of legal obligations to verify mileage and describe the car accurately. Discovering if you have found a closet trader is common sense and give-aways will be a slick manner, unconvincing reasons for selling and more than one car for sale when you call. Maybe the seller wants to meet somewhere other than at their home. That is the sort of person you need to avoid.

THE QUESTIONS YOU MUST ASK

Most of us will respond to advertisements by telephone and that's a good idea. By all means email a list of questions, but primarily get on the phone at some point so that you can make a decision not just about the car, but crucially the seller. If they are hesitant, or evasive and you don't like their tone, what's the point? Call it all off and save yourself a wasted journey.

Repeat the advert – Yes really, you must confirm that the details are correct and that there are no printing errors.
Mileage? Clarify precise miles, as some ads just say 'average'.

Service records? You need to know if the miles can be backed up by real evidence.

First Registered? When was the car built which helps confirm which model it is.

MOT/Annual Inspection expiry? Some ads say 'long', or 'short' MOT.

Can the car be examined by an engineer? If the seller is reluctant, they can't be confident about their car.

Any warranties/guarantees? The seller might have an existing guarantee for a replacement engine, battery, etc.

Car tax/Number plate expiry? Also is it included in the price? Most sellers, including the trade, cash in the tax unless they agree otherwise.

Owned the car long? If a private seller has only had it a few weeks, maybe there is something wrong.

What's wrong with it? Be specific; ask about engine, bodywork, and interior. Many sellers give amazingly honest replies, others will be evasive.

Modified? A tuned engine or spoilers could change your opinion of the car, not to mention the insurance quote.

Previous owners? Less the better, obviously. Where did you buy it? Private buyer should be able to say where it came from, for instance a family member, dealer etc

Registration documents? A private seller should at least have a receipt and certainly a registration document as proof of ownership. If there is no paperwork, be suspicious, or don't bother.

Is the car on finance? If so, the outstanding money on the loan must to be paid off before you buy otherwise you won't own the car, the finance company will.

Can I have the registration number and VIN (Vehicle Identification Number) of the car? This means you can get the car data checked against a vehicle database, which operates in some countries. It will reveal whether the car is stolen, an insurance write off, or not what the seller says it is. If they are not keen on giving you information maybe they have something to hide.

Why are you selling? Private seller should have a quick and convincing answer.

Can I test drive the car? No point turning up if you can't do this.

Do Think carefully about the answers given and decide whether or not the car is worth following up. You don't have to agree to see the car right away, you can always call the seller back later after giving it some serious thought.

Don't Agree to meet the seller halfway at a motorway service area. Maybe the car isn't theirs to sell. Always make an appointment to view the car in daylight, because looking at a car with a torch or by touch is not recommended.

So you think you like the sound of the answers and the sound of the car? In that case you move on with confidence to the next chapter, but not before doing your coursework.

Browsing for Bangers – Coursework

Go Exploring
What you have to do is look at as many used cars for sale as you can and consider all the different buying options too. Never been to an auction? Go and have a look. Car dealers? Spend a weekend wandering around car lots and car supermarkets. Or just phoning them up, because you will learn so much.

Get Chatting
Respond to some ads even if you don't want the car, see how far your questioning gets you and just what you can find out.

6

Bang Splutter Clang

Banger Checks

IT IS NOW TIME for Bangernomics students to get their hands dirty. As daunting as it may seem there is no reason to be frightened by the prospect of checking a car out. What must be established is that the vehicle is suitable and sound enough for your purposes; then you can call in the experts if you want to. So the initial once over is down to you because there is no point in paying for professional checks on every Banger you like the look of.

Don't worry, even if you are mechanically bewildered, because the Bangernomics approach is straightforward enough for anyone with the minimum amount of common sense and reasonable powers of observation to make an informed and accurate decision. You will be told why you are doing something and not simply given a bizarre set of confusing rituals, which could embarrass everyone. As a first step to gaining confidence why not carry out the tests in this chapter on a friend's car? Then you will know how long it takes and how simple the tests are to perform. You might be able to tell your friend the true condition of their Banger.

The point has been made to me over the years that you are better off not looking at a car as that can compromise your legal rights if anything is wrong. Now I don't see the point of buying a Banger with your eyes shut and hoping for the best. If you are buying from a private seller the chances of getting any money back or a successful prosecution are marginal. It is amazing what you can spot just by looking. Even if you reckon the car is OK, the final car checks before buying should always be left to a mechanically qualified professional for complete peace of mind.

And finally, you may not be looking at a car as we used to understand it. Maybe it hovers, or travels at the speed of light, in which case what follows is utterly irrelevant. Well actually the basic principles should be the same. That at the very least you bother to turn up and check what you are buying. Plus if it makes a strange noise, looks rough and handles like a lame carthorse (a reference there to what came before the horseless carriage as it used to be called), then you will have spotted a PTD, Personal Transportation Device, that isn't worth buying.

BANGER SURVIVAL KIT

CLOTHES: You should dress appropriately and that means scruffily. Any clothing that might be improved by the odd oil stain would be ideal. If you have sensitive hands, or would rather not get them dirty, don't be afraid to wear gloves. These should be fairly thin – don't bother with mittens – but rubber gloves allow you to poke around more easily and you can also buy thin latex disposable ones. There is also the psychological factor that if you do resemble a tramp, then the seller really believes it when you plead poverty and offer to pay less than they are asking.

RAGS: No, these are not your clothes but a couple of very useful items that may have started life as your underwear. You can use them to kneel on when looking around the car, when checking the oil, or just to help you wipe away the grime when trying to get a better look at something.

MAGNET: You can still pick them up in toy shops, or why not simply pinch one of those daft things that live on the door of

EXHIBIT

your refrigerator. What a magnet does is stick to metal and drop off any replacement fibreglass panels or filler and it is also reluctant to cling to rust. Rust isn't such a big issue in more modern Bangers, but you should be prepared.

TORCH: Helps you get a good look underneath the car, in wheel arches, even in the boot and under the bonnet. Make sure it works before you leave.

MIRROR: Not absolutely essential, but useful in allowing you to see into awkward places.

SCREWDRIVER/METAL PEN: This is for poking around with (always ask the seller's permission first), so it need not be a brand new item and an old metal pen looks less threatening.

CLIPBOARD: Guaranteed to strike fear into any dodgy seller. Even if you don't feel professional, it will at least make you look as though you know what you are doing. With that clipboard you should also have a pen and the check sheets in the BANGLOSSARY. This will take you through the tests in this chapter and help you assess the condition of the car.

FRIEND: This item is particularly important because they can give an objective view of the car, for example: "What a heap, you're not buying that are you? You cannot be serious, get a grip" etc. Just as importantly they can also distract the seller (by chatting to them) so that you can examine the car unhindered. Of course it may help if the friend knows something about cars, but that is by no means essential. They are also useful as a human tape recorder to witness the exaggerations of the seller when they swear on their mother's life that the car is A1, or that they will give you some money off.

BANGERNOMICS BIBLE: Yes that's right, keep this copy of Bangernomics up your sleeve, or in your pocket as a useful reference before doing battle with the seller.

INSURANCE: Just a final reminder that when buying privately you must have some insurance cover for the test drive. However, dealers must have cover for you to drive and if they do not, something is wrong.

The First Five Minutes

EARLY: It is a good idea to get to the seller's residence or forecourt early. Identify the car and then have a good look around before attracting the seller's attention. You might be able to make an instant decision; so make your excuses and leave. Alternatively, you might catch the seller trying to kick it into life. Also, ensure that you are there early enough in the day to see the car in the light. An amazing number of people are apparently happy to pay good money for a car they could only feel in the twilight. Don't make this fundamental mistake. Just as importantly establish that this is where the seller lives. Believe it or not some sellers park outside a house and pretend they live there. It may be to impress you, but mostly it is to mislead you, especially if the car isn't theirs to sell. If you have any doubts invent an excuse to go into the house, so ask the seller for a glass of water or to use their toilet.

TIME: You are the customer and, as we know, customers are always right. The car might be cheap, but that is no reason why you should be rushed around it in five minutes and then be asked whether or not you want to buy. Take your time.

CAR: The first thing to organise is that the car can be clearly seen. If it is parked on a forecourt, this often means that they are squeezed in door to door, or a private seller may simply open a garage door and invite you to squeeze around it, which is not good enough. Only when you can see the car clearly can you begin to make your first checks.

QUESTIONS: This is a good time to recap the questions you should have asked over the telephone/email, especially relating to the car's condition. In the flesh, sellers start to 'remember' all sorts of fascinating facts about the car, like the time it went for a swim in the North Sea. If the life story of the car is changing too rapidly and significantly, then perhaps you should back out before wasting too much time.

PAPERWORK: The good news is that you are not going to get your hands dirty straight away. What you need to establish is that the car is as described and that the owner really does own it.

REGISTRATION/OWNERSHIP DOCUMENT: In many countries you can't get the annual road tax, or get a new registration plate without a slip of paper indicating ownership. So if the seller does not have this legal document, be suspicious. The car could be stolen, the document could be with a finance company because they actually own the car. Don't ever buy a used car without getting the genuine document. So make sure that it is. Look at it very closely. Are there any spelling mistakes or alterations? If so, it may be a forgery. Assuming it is still a physical document, hold it up to the light as legitimate documents usually have watermarks. If it is a credit card then a hologram will probably be built in. If checking online, make sure you are on the official government run website. This document establishes the identity of the owner in front of you, or if you are dealing with a dealer, the previous owner. However, the person named as the registered keeper is not necessarily the legal owner.

If the car is being sold privately does the name and address on the document correspond with the person selling it? Ask for proof of the seller's identity and address such as a driving licence, passport, or electricity bill. Check that the same name and address is given on the document. When buying from a dealer, record the previous owner's name and address, you may want to make contact with them later. Note the number of previous owners and the date of the last sale. Perhaps this is a troublesome car being sold in quick succession? As mentioned previously, the fewer the number of owners the more likely it has been looked after.

Write down the date of registration, colour, model description (GTi, GL, etc) engine and chassis or VIN (vehicle identification numbers) so that you can check it against the car itself. So look at the vehicle registration mark (the number plate) and VIN – this can be found on a metal plate in the engine compartment usually where the bonnet closes at the front, and stamped into the bodywork under the bonnet. Some cars also have the VIN etched on their windows, lamps, or mounted behind the windscreen on the top of the dashboard. The engine number is usually stamped on a prominent part of the engine. These numbers on the car should be the same as those on the registration document. Even if they match, have the numbers been tampered with? Areas of glass may have been scratched off the windows, or stickers may cover up an etching, which has been altered. This is usually done to hide the identity of a stolen car. When in doubt ask the seller for their insurance documents. When the car is stolen it is unlikely that they will have any insurance documents, although even these can be forged.

BILL OF SALE/ORIGINAL RECEIPT: Should the registration/ownership document be inconclusive, perhaps the seller has proof that the car was purchased and has the receipt to prove it. Maybe you can trace this back to the dealer or person that sold it. If the details are very different from the registration document maybe you should forget this vehicle.

SERVICE HISTORY/BILLS: These are reassuring pieces of paper, which could prove that the car has been looked after and could back the seller's claim that they recently spent 'a fortune'. What you want to see is a folder, or file full of history rather than some apologetic slips of paper or just a stamped up service book which can be forged anyway.

Read through them carefully because you must establish that they relate to the same vehicle. Do the stamps in a service book look like they were applied at the same time? If so they may be forged. If there are garage details write them down and then contact the garage and ask them about the car. Another good reason for looking through them is that there may be a receipt which says the car was completely rebuilt after being damaged or was repaired after a flood. So **READ THEM.** They will tell you when the cam belt was changed. If it has not been done the belt will snap and wreck the engine.

ROADWORTHINESS CERTIFICATE: In some countries cars are inspected every year to ensure they are safe. However, just because the car has a current test certificate is no guarantee that the car is roadworthy. To guard against this note the mileage recorded at the time of the last test and compare it with the reading on the mileometer. If someone has been fiddling with the mileage reading that will be obvious, it should also give you an idea of the average mileage, especially if there are several certificates to compare. Also cross-reference the details such  as registration, cc (cubic capacity of the engine), date of manufacture and VIN numbers with that on the Registration Document. If you have doubts about the certificate's validity you may be able to check it online.

ROAD FUND LICENCE/REGISTRATION PLATE: Check that it is valid, it must be if you are going to test-drive the car.

THE CAR: You've done the easy bit and if you are happy with what you have read then you can move onto the car itself. Also refer to the BANGING ABOUT chapter for more information on how a car should operate if it is properly maintained and what the signs may be if there are problems.

IN THE OPEN: As mentioned earlier get the car out into the open, in daylight and ideally in dry weather. Rain does strange things to paintwork and can make it look brighter than it really is. Walk away to a distance of between 12 to 15ft (4-5 metres). Look at the car from the front, rear and both sides. Does the car sit square on the road? If not, is a tyre deflated, or is the road surface uneven? Can't find fault with the tyre or surface? Then this may indicate that the suspension is close to, or has actually collapsed. Alternatively it points to a car that may have been haphazardly bolted back together after an accident. If you feel that the car could be dangerous to drive, then don't.

KEEP YOUR DISTANCE: Do the panels look even and are they damaged? By looking along the sides of the car, from both the front and rear you can see the real condition of the bodywork. Misaligned panels, ripples and general unevenness again suggest that the car has been rebuilt after an accident. You may also be able to see any differences in the paintwork colour, so has the car been resprayed? Ask why.

GET CLOSER: Do any of the panels look as though they need to be replaced, or simply bear the scars of careless parking? In particular look at the paintwork, especially if you noticed any contrast in the colours when standing back, inspect them more closely. Old paintwork fades and any touch-ups should be obvious. You might see some drips, flecks of fresh paint or a matt surface. A cheap paint job means that there will be evidence of overspray (paint) on the window rubbers, under the wheel arches and on the tyres. The fact that this has been done is not important, but the reason why it has been done is crucial and that means it is time to ask the seller. Has the car just been brightened up to justify a higher than average price? Perhaps some major rust or damage has been camouflaged. Ask.

OPEN AND CLOSE: all the doors, boot and bonnet, do they fit snugly, or snag on the surrounding metal and do the locks work?

RUST HUNT: Now you are nice and close, this is the time to start looking for rust. Improvements in bodywork protection means that it may no longer be a major issue unless there have been poor repairs after an accident. With older classic cars though rust is still very much an issue and it will be the difference between buying and looking for another car in much better condition. Otherwise the nasty little rust bug starts at the bottom of the car where moisture and water collects and then eats its way upwards through the bodywork. What you have to distinguish between is serious and superficial rust. The car may be full of holes but it can still be perfectly legal. Generally, minor rust on the

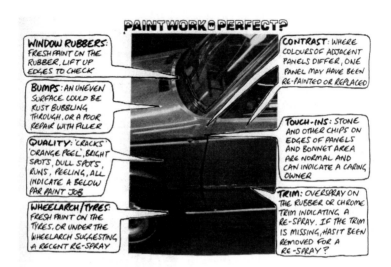

PAINTWORK PERFECT?

WINDOW RUBBERS: FRESH PAINT ON THE RUBBER, LIFT UP EDGES TO CHECK

BUMPS: AN UNEVEN SURFACE COULD BE RUST BUBBLING THROUGH, OR A POOR REPAIR WITH FILLER

QUALITY: 'CRACKS' 'ORANGE PEEL', BRIGHT SPOTS, DULL SPOTS, RUNS, PEELING, ALL INDICATE A BELOW PAR PAINT JOB

WHEELARCH/TYRES: FRESH PAINT ON THE TYRES, OR UNDER THE WHEELARCH SUGGESTING A RECENT RE-SPRAY

CONTRAST: WHERE COLOURS OF ADJACENT PANELS DIFFER, ONE PANEL MAY HAVE BEEN RE-PAINTED OR REPLACED

TOUCH-INS: STONE AND OTHER CHIPS ON EDGES OF PANELS AND BONNET AREA ARE NORMAL AND CAN INDICATE A CARING OWNER

TRIM: OVERSPRAY ON THE RUBBER OR CHROME TRIM INDICATING A RE-SPRAY. IF THE TRIM IS MISSING, HAS IT BEEN REMOVED FOR A RE-SPRAY?

edges of panels is rarely serious, so a rusty bonnet, doors and wings can easily be lived with, or simply repaired. However, structural rust is more serious making the car unsafe and unroadworthy as the important load bearing areas of the car can no longer take the strain. The problem is that whereas most mechanical parts can be easily and cheaply replaced, serious rot is too uneconomic to repair, requiring hours of intensive rebuilding work. So if you think that the rust is serious then forget about the car.

MAGNET: This will not stick to rusted or filled areas and replacement plastic body panels. If you suspect any area, be subtle with a magnet (put it in your palm) and cover it with a layer of paper so that it does not damage the paintwork. Be aware that some cars may have some plastic panels as standard, especially tailgates.

HANDS: These are very sensitive instruments indeed. Running the palm over the bodywork can pick up imperfections and filler very quickly. Press any suspect parts of a panel with your fingers and feel for any give, which suggests filler, or rust underneath, especially if you hear a 'cracking' sound.

UNDERSIDE: Don't get underneath the car. Don't even jack it up. Even if you have axle stands. Examining the underside of a car should only be done in a workshop. However you may just be able to see some important parts by lying next to it and using your torch. Leave the complete underside inspection to the experts but you may just spot some very obvious fault.

RUST HUNT

▲ WINDSCREEN PILLAR

SERIOUS ROT

SUSPENSION ▲ MOUNTS

SERIOUS ROT

SILLS ▼

▼ INNER WINGS

COSMETIC RUST
► EDGES OF PANELS
► AROUND HEADLAMPS
► WINGS
► WHEEL ARCHES
► AROUND TRIM, AERIALS ETC
► BOTTOM OF DOORS

SCREWDRIVER/METAL PEN: Not to be plunged into the bodywork as the seller is likely to get upset, but it is useful to clean away mud and muck to see if there is rot underneath. The screwdriver is also excellent to tap suspect bits of metal. If you hear a pleasing ring, or resonate sound then it may be solid enough, but a dull thud that absorbs the tap rather than bouncing off it indicates rust and possibly filler.

1. SILLS: The nearest thing to you when you get on the floor are the sills. These must be solid. Also the sills can sustain damage, especially on off road vehicles that are grounded, so this can tell you something about how the car has been used and possibly abused.

2. SUSPENSION: Attached to the wheels and usually bolted to the bodywork is the suspension. You may see some leaks from shock absorbers (tubes behind wheels), which means they need replacing. Can you see any parts that seem bent or out of true, or just rotten?

3. EXHAUST: There are tests you can perform with the engine running (see further), but for the moment look at the silencer boxes and pipes, are they attached firmly to the car, are they rotten or crudely patched up? Some of these boxes can be replaced individually. If the exhaust looks new, or is made of stainless steel (which lasts the life of the car), you are in luck and it points to a caring owner. The catalytic converter (which cleans up the fumes) can be damaged but this is not always obvious from a visual check, again see further in the test drive section.

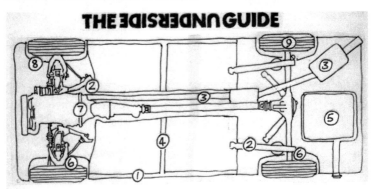

THE UNDERSIDE GUIDE

4. FLOOR: Now look at the floor and the cross sections of metal, again you are searching for rot and signs of poor and obvious repairs. If something looks wrong then it probably is. Patches and fresh underseal all suggest a recent and possibly substandard repair.

5. PETROL TANK: At the rear of the car you may be able to see the fuel tank. On older models these can rot badly (modern tanks are plastic), resulting in leaks. Any suspiciously clean part would signal trouble as fuel is an excellent remover of dirt and grime. Follow the petrol line to the front of the car if you can to check leaks and condition. Obviously a strong smell of petrol indicates that there may be a leak.

6. BRAKES: The thin pipes leading from the rear wheels to the front are the brake pipes. These should be intact, rust free and showing no fluid leaks. There are also flexible pipes that you may be able to see on every wheel hub (onto which the wheel is bolted).

7. OIL LEAKS: Use the ground to help you. If the car is parked on its usual spot (in the street this is difficult to know, but the parking spot on the seller's property is more conclusive) then you should be able to see any oily evidence on the ground. The engine area is the obvious place to shine your torch. Also on cars that have rear wheel drive and 4x4 vehicles follow the big tube (propshaft) to the rear axle differential (T junction with the wheels at either end). If there are any shiny and oily items, then you may have spotted a leak. Minor leaks on older cars give little cause for concern, but if oil seals need replacing, this could be expensive.

8. WHEEL ARCHES: As you happen to be at ground level you might as well have a peek inside where the wheels are kept. These are favourite places for mud and grunge to collect which will eventually rot the metal. Have a good poke around and be suspicious if there is any freshly applied dirt, or possibly sticky black underseal paint that could be covering up any recent repairs.

9. TYRES: Whilst you are on the outside, take a good look at the tyres. These are important items as they are all that keep you on the road. Also much of the car's braking and cornering ability is lost if the tyres are badly worn, leading to prosecution in some countries. Tyre faults include, having incorrect pressures, cuts, lumps or bulges, exposed cord or ply and badly worn tread. A tyre that wears on the inner or outer surface indicates that the wheel is not vertical or directly in line with the one behind it. A tyre that wears in the middle or has bulges has probably been over inflated. If all that sounds a bit too complicated just remember that cuts, bald spots, bulges and mixtures of tyre types are all bad news and require sorting out. When in doubt don't risk a test drive until that tyre has been replaced. Without getting too complicated, all the information you need is written on the tyre wall itself, telling you its type, the manufacturer and maximum pressure. Personally I like to see the same make of tyre on all wheels, which indicates an owner who cared.

10. BOOT: Open it and look inside, it's amazing what you may find in there. Water and moisture can collect in the nooks and crevices of the boot, so move the rubbish out of the way and look for rust. Remove the spare wheel, and look where it has been sitting, a pool of water suggests a leaky boot and probably a rotten floor section. The boot area can also show signs of repair, especially if the car has been hit hard from behind and repair sections have been welded in. The floor may also look rippled. Then check the spare wheel and tyre for condition. These can be neglected and in poor condition. Also if the battery is located here, inspect the area surrounding it, as spilled acid will start corrosion (the battery can also be under the rear seats). Is there a wheel brace and jack for changing a wheel? If you are very lucky you may find a tool kit and a warning triangle.

INTERIOR: Now you can find out even more about how the car has been looked after, or not.

FLOOR/CARPETS: Try and lift the carpets, in many modern cars this is not possible, but on older classics where rot is going to be an issue it is crucial to look under there. So can you see the road through the floor? A musty smell and damp carpets, accompanied with condensation on the windows, also points to lots of water inside which means rotting bodywork. With all cars look at the carpets closely. Maybe someone had an accident in there once and maybe spilt a bottle of milk. Many stains and smells can't be shifted so lift up the over carpets.

WINDOWS: Wind them up and down (or press the buttons), do they all work? Then turn your attention to the panes themselves, if security etched with the vehicle number, do they match the number plates? If not, why not? A close look at the windscreen from both inside and out could reveal a number of scratches and cracks. If serious the windscreen will need to be replaced. Try asking the owner to replace it under their insurance policy, this is well worth a try especially if the crack is bad.

SEATS/SEATBELTS: Remove any covers and assess the seats for comfort and condition. In particular, does the driver's seat adjust? Look at the seatbelts, the webbing must not be frayed or broken, and the anchor points (where they attach to the body) must be secure.

MILEAGE: It would be nice to know the true mileage of the car you are considering although the most important factor is always the actual condition. Far better to have a high mileage car, which has been regularly serviced than a low mile one that has only gone to the shops occasionally. Short journeys will cumulatively kill a car's engine. But if the mileage is claimed to be very low, or the seller is asking you to pay more for the car because of how well it has been looked after, then it is worth checking further. Few sellers would ever go to the trouble of renewing the interior to hide the true mileage of a car, so if the paperwork did not convince you that the mileage was genuine you can find more clues in here and spot a high miler.

- Tug on the driver's seatbelt and then let go. If it snaps back fine. If it takes forever to retract the car has done a big mileage.
- Squashy, frayed and worn driver's seat? More signs that there have been lots of bums on seats.
- A worn and shiny steering wheel, a worn and equally shiny gear knob, where the gear pattern is fading, an ignition key which has rounded edges, worn pedal rubbers and also a hole in the driver's side carpet are all signs that the car has done at least 100,000 miles.
- Look at the dashboard. Are the screws holding it in place worn, or scratched? Does the steering wheel look out of alignment? If so someone may have been trying to get at the mileometer to adjust the miles. On older cars the mileometer numbers may not be level

suggesting an alteration. With electronic digital readouts it is impossible to tell if it has been altered by a rogue with a lap top computer. The only confirmation of the true mileage is the paperwork and the condition of the interior.

- As mentioned before contact the previous owner whose address is on the V5 registration document and ask for the mileage when they sold it.

LIGHTS: Use your friend positioned outside to check that all the lights work, front and rear from the indicators and headlamps through to stop lights and also any additional lamps such as fog or driving lights.

CONTROLS: Push, pull and prod all the relevant switches and knobs to make sure that the radio, electric windows, and sunroof all work. Electrical faults can be difficult to remedy and are very annoying. It may be something as simple as a blown fuse, then again it might not be.

Windscreen Wipers and washers: Legally they must work, so even if it is not raining, don't be afraid to try them out.

Dashboard: Switch on the ignition and you should find a lot of lights flashing at you and/or gauges indicating something or other. Some are more important than others. **Oil:** This is usually a red light, often accompanied by an oil can or dipstick symbol. Ideally it comes on with the ignition but goes out within a second of the engine starting telling you there is enough oil in the system to lubricate the engine. If the light stays on, then there is engine trouble. **Ignition:** This light may have 'IGN', or a battery symbol below it.

Not surprisingly it comes on when the ignition is switched on but if it remains alight then either the battery or charging system is faulty. **Brake:** A red or yellow light for both the foot and handbrake. The handbrake light will go off when disengaged. However, if the light flickers then the brake fluid may need to be topped up. Some cars have brake pad wear lights and if they need replacement the light will stay on. When in doubt consult the owner's manual if it still exists, often located in the glove box, a good seller will still have it. **ABS:** Many cars have anti-skid brakes and the light should come on and go off very quickly otherwise there may be a problem with the system.

Air conditioning: It may be a simple manually controlled system or a more complicated climate control system that operates automatically. Essentially it should blow hot and cold. When in doubt though it should be checked by an air conditioning specialist. It may simply need some more refrigerant gas or perhaps the sensors are not working properly. It could also be a pump or compressor or some other part which is very expensive to sort out. This is Bangernomics though and we really should not care whether the car blows hot and cold, we just want the engine and gearbox to work.

OILY BITS: This is the part that some Bangernomics students think they might just flunk, frightened by the technology. However, there is nothing scary under the bonnet and although the mechanics of the modern motor car can be complex, there is no need to know which does what, in order to spot a fault. It is a simple case of keeping eyes and ears open. A few words of warning though, if you have not put your cigarette out, do it now. Also, tuck away any items of loose clothing and tie back long hair if you don't want to become an integral part of a whirling engine. Don't forget that an engine gets very hot so keep unprotected fingers away. **Note:** If the car has been warmed up before you arrive the seller may have something to hide, perhaps it is difficult to start, or it makes strange noises when cold.

SUSPENSION/STEERING:

The bodywork checks, especially when you looked underneath, might already have revealed any strengths or weaknesses in the suspension. Mainly these relate to corrosion and leaks. By peering into the wheel arches you should be able to see if there is any fluid leaking from the shock absorbers and possibly corroded suspension springs.

Many engineers will tell you that mileage and age are important factors in assessing their condition. After a decade's use and/or 80-100,000 miles it is probably time that the shock absorbers were replaced. However the bounce test (which is not conclusive) does give a good indication of the suspension's effectiveness. Simply push down on the wing above each wheel, the car should bounce straight back then settle on the down stroke. If it keeps bouncing, the shock absorbers definitely need replacing.

Put some gloves on and grasp the front road wheel and push it forwards and backwards, to see if there is any play in the suspension, especially if you hear any clonks or knocks (note: certain makes of cars have unique suspension systems, when expert help would be needed). Now rock it against the steering (pull and push) listening for clonks and watching for any play in the steering.

Put your hands on the steering wheel and move it slightly, is there any play (no more than an inch/2.5 cm), or movement before the road wheels turn? Your friend can help here. If there is play, then the steering may be worn, which the test drive should confirm. This will affect the roadworthiness of the car and it may need a specialist to investigate further.

UNDER THE BONNET: Don't start the engine yet, first of all try and assess the condition of the compartment. Anything that looks shiny and new is a bonus, but does it back up what the owner has already told you? If it looks dirty in there, that is the least of your worries. Of course a tidy and well-kept area would suggest a caring owner. However, dealers and owners who steam clean the engine might well end up with a surface that you could eat sandwiches off, but it can remove evidence of neglect. Steam cleaning can also cause problems with vehicle electrics and may explain why some warning lights are on.

UNPLUGGED?: Hitching a car up to an electronic diagnostic system is a simple option to find out if there are any fault codes that could explain what's wrong. As you may be reading this in the future you may be able to do this through a computer programme or a mobile phone. If it is an option then use it.

COVERED?: Many modern engine compartments have huge covers on them. This is done partly to tidy up the appearance but it also stops the untrained and unwashed amateurs like us prodding around. What you can touch is often helpfully coloured in bright yellow. Otherwise on certain models it can be difficult to see very much under there.

OIL: Look first for leaks around the engine block and gearbox. Get on your knees and look at the engine from underneath, especially the sump (a rectangular box at the base of the engine) where the oil lives. Move the car or wander back to where it was previously parked, is there an oil slick on the spot? Remove the oil filler cap and look for creamy deposits, which suggests water mixing with the oil, this is bad news.

Ensuring that the car is on level ground, take out the dipstick (a metal rod mounted on the side or middle of the engine often with a yellow lid or end), wipe it with your cloth, re-insert and withdraw again. The level should be somewhere between the max and min marks. Too low and the car has probably not been cared for. The condition of the oil on the end of the stick tells its own story. New oil is gold and clear, like honey. Normally used oil is darker but you should still be able to see the end of the stick. Dirty black oil points to a car that has rarely been serviced. The presence of tiny bubbles suggests that water is starting to mix with the oil, this usually happens when the head gasket blows. This is another problem you don't need.

Look for the oil filter; this is a brightly coloured cylinder, which screws into the side of the engine block. If it looks old and filthy, basic servicing procedures may have been skipped.

WATER: Now take off the radiator cap, or cap on the plastic expansion tank which is to one side of the engine bay (only to be done with a cold, never a hot engine) and look at the water. Once again whitish deposits point to oil and water mixing. Put your fingers in, and then rub them together; do they feel oily? During winter especially, there should be anti-freeze in the cooling system, which turns the water blue, green or red. Orange water suggests that there is rust in the system, which in turn damages a lot of components. If you can't see any water there may be a leak in the system. Look below to see if there are any drips and check the condition of the hoses, do they look old, perished and cracked? Orange stains are the give-away to water leaks which suggests poor maintenance. Brownish stains, which may even discolour the inside of the bonnet, indicate that the car has overheated due either to a blocked system, failing water pump, or blown head gasket. This could happen again.

BATTERY: Find it first; most are under the bonnet, some in the boot whilst the odd few can be located under the back seat. Almost all batteries are now sealed for life, but with any other type, take off the six filler caps and check the distilled water level which should just cover the metal elements. Check the terminals, the metal posts at either end of the battery, these corrode and become covered in white powder, which can hamper its effectiveness and explain poor starting.

GEARBOX: Initially you can check the gearbox without the engine running and just make sure that the gear lever moves smoothly into all of the gears. Then start the car. The lever must not vibrate, which is a sign of wear. More simple tests can be performed on the move.

START ENGINE: At last you can start the car. Ask the seller how it is done, there may be a procedure you are not familiar with or some rigmarole you have to go through to get past the immobiliser/alarm. Position your tame friend at the rear of the car, ensure the gearbox is in neutral and turn the key. Does it start easily? A slow turnover or several attempts could point to a weak battery. Do all of the warning lights go out? If something is flashing at you find out what that light refers too. Listen carefully (q.v. Nail that Noise). Now get out of the car and ask your friend if they saw any white or dark blue smoke on start-up? An old car is allowed a little puff to begin with, but a constant plume of smoke indicates that there could be serious problems.

APPLY BRAKES: Push the brake pedal, it should feel firm and not immediately descend to the floor. It's essential to know they are operational before hitting the road and then maybe a wall.

ENGAGE CLUTCH: With the engine running depress the clutch, it should move smoothly and silently, a whirring noise points to a worn release bearing. Engage second gear and the handbrake, increase the revs and let the clutch out. If the car stalls with the revs dropping rapidly then it is OK. Otherwise the clutch is slipping and may have to be replaced.

NAIL THAT NOISE

WHISTLING LEAK IN CARBURETTOR OR INLET MANIFOLD. ALSO CHUFFING POINTS TO MANIFOLD WITH A PROBLEM.

TICKING FROM MIDDLE. BROKEN PISTON RING. CAN BE A COSTLY GARAGE JOB.

KNOCK FROM MIDDLE WHICH SUBSIDES ONCE ENGINE WARM NO PROBLEM, CALLED 'PISTON SLAP', PROVIDED OIL LEVEL IS CORRECT.

REMEMBER ANY PROBLEM COULD ALSO BE A COMPUTER CHIP

RUMBLING ROTATING NOISE FROM LOWER PART OF ENGINE, WORN MAIN BEARINGS, ENGINE REBUILD NEEDED.

TAPPING AT THE TOP. COULD SIMPLY NEED VALVE ADJUSTMENT. OVERHEAD VALVE CARS COULD HAVE WORN ROCKER ARM OR SHAFT. OVERHEAD CAMSHAFT ENGINES COULD HAVE WORN CAMSHAFTS

HARD KNOCK FROM BOTTOM, WORN BIG END BEARINGS. REBUILD ENGINE.

HISSING, LEAKING WATER PUMP OR HOSE. SIMPLE TO REPAIR, BUT COOLING SYSTEM MAY NEED TO BE CHECKED. **BUBBLING** – **THUMP** FROM THIS AREA COULD BE OVERHEATING DUE TO HEAD GASKET AND THERMOSTAT FAILURE. DON'T DRIVE, CHECK WATER LEVEL WHEN COOL

RUMBLING FROM FRONT END, WORN WATER PUMP OR ALTERNATOR BEARING, EASY TO REPLACE, CHECK PARTS PRICES FIRST.

SCHREECHING ESPECIALLY WHEN ENGINE REVVED – SLACK FAN BELT. **WHINING** – TOO TIGHT, BOTH EASY TO CURE

RATTLING FROM FRONT END INDICATES WORN OR LOOSE TIMING CHAIN. STRAIGHTFORWARD GARAGE JOB ON MOST CARS

AUTOMATIC GEARBOX: Check that the gearbox lever moves smoothly into each gear. Then with the engine running and brakes on perform the same checks, the engine should not rev when the changes are made, and ideally the operation is silent and smooth. Then, with your foot firmly on the foot brake engage D (Drive) and lightly press the accelerator, then engage R (Reverse). In both cases the car should rise up against the brakes and not stall.

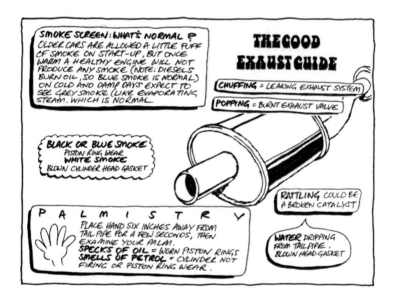

DIESEL: Never drive a warmed-up diesel, always start from cold to make sure it starts easily. Difficulty starting indicates that the engine may be worn and losing compression, which is bad. Also the heavy-duty battery may be losing power and is unable to turn the engine. Be wary of an oily engine bay which could be spraying fluid from the breather pipes, indicating severe wear. These pipes connect with the air cleaner, a box on the top of the engine. Also examine the diesel injector, pump and pipe work where it connects to the engine for leaks as it operates under very high pressure and is crucial to efficient performance and replacement is costly. Basically leaks are bad.

FOUR-WHEEL DRIVE: It is crucial to examine the bodywork and underside of the vehicle, especially if it is taken off-road. Look for dents, twisted chassis, suspension and corrosion. Find out how the four-wheel drive system works and then use it. Listen for noises from front and rear driveshafts and the transmission. Lots of grinding noises is bad news.

TURBOS: Fitted to many high performance cars and the vast majority of modern diesel engines. Best guarantee of good health is a full service history. Often it is hard to spot a turbo going on the blink, but look out for lots of blue smoke when accelerating hard.

TEST DRIVE: Having established that the car is in your judgement safe and legal and provided you have no second thoughts or doubts, make it clear to the seller that you want to take the car for a test drive. This should not be a simple spin around the block, but a proper drive of at least 10 miles and half an hour minimum. If they object then make your excuses and leave, or at least offer to pay for the fuel used. However, if you have had a problem getting insurance at short notice, or the owner is so protective of their car that they will not let you drive, all is not lost. If the owner follows your route and carries out the tests according to your instructions then go along with it. This means that you will have to watch what they do very carefully, as some drivers will attempt to disguise a fault. But if they carry out these tests and you keep your eyes and ears open there is no reason why you should miss a major problem.

The idea is to cover as many different types of motoring conditions as possible, from dual carriageway to town driving. Before moving off and provided the seller agrees, install your friend in the car as an extra pair of eyes and ears. If the radio is on, turn it off because it could hide noises and open a window so that you can hear what is going on outside. Don't treat the car as your own and tell the seller before you carry out any test what you are doing. Remember to keep an eye out for flicking warning lights, or oil pressure and water temperature gauges (when fitted) that seem to be very active.

FIRST DRIVING IMPRESSIONS: Once the car is warmed up, engage the gears and pull sharply away. If there is an audible 'clonk', on rear wheel drive cars (rear wheels powered) this could mean that the propshaft needs replacing, a major garage job. When accelerating, the car should not jump out of gear, otherwise it needs attention. An automatic gearbox should change smoothly and quietly. Compared of course, to the kind of car you are used to, does it feel sluggish? It may be that the engine needs a simple service and minor adjustment,

or it could be that the engine is about to expire. Only a few more tests will tell.

CLUTCH CHECK: With a manual transmission model drive up a hill (it does not have to be very steep) and accelerate; again the car should not jump out of gear. Stop and apply the handbrake, then put your foot on the brake and release it slowly. Does it hold? Perform a hill start and see how the car reacts, especially the clutch.

SMOKE ALERT: When descending the hill leave the car in gear and take your foot off the accelerator, then provided it is safe, at the bottom, accelerate away. In the rear view mirror you may see a puff of smoke, but not a smokescreen. A smokescreen means a badly worn engine in need of an overhaul.

CATACLYSMIC: Catalytic Converters are vital but expensive components of the exhaust system and they can fail at any time. You may hear rattling in the exhaust (internal breakages) and notice that the acceleration is poor (blocked cat). Damage is often caused as a result of an incorrect air/fuel mixture, incorrect timing, or misfiring spark plugs, which could all lead to a catalytic converter failure.

TAKE A BRAKE: Find a quiet road with no one about and at about 30 mph perform an emergency stop. There is no need to slam the brakes on, just apply them firmly. The car should stop in a straight line. If anything dramatic happens, like you start  to go excitingly sideways, release the brake and steer your way out of trouble. End the test-drive if you feel unsafe, but bear in mind that brake problems can usually be sorted out fairly easily and quickly by a garage. Should the brakes squeal it could be a simple case of lubrication for a disc brake or, more seriously, worn wheel bearings, whilst drum brakes (fitted to the rear of older cars) could be very badly worn.

SOUND ENGINE: Now pull away with the car in second gear, or alternatively, slow right down and then accelerate in fourth. A sound engine will not jerk, stall or make any ominous knocking sounds.

STEER CLEAR: Ensuring that you are on a quiet road, bring the speed up to 30 mph and loosen your grip on the steering wheel. If the car pulls noticeably to one side there may be something wrong with the suspension, or an indication that the chassis is twisted after an accident. However, there could also be a very simple explanation such as incorrect tyre pressures.

SUSPENDED ANIMATION: Find some rough ground, or aim the car at some all too common potholes, does the vehicle pitch and wallow, taking some time to settle down? The suspension

could be worn, confirming the results of the bounce test, which you should have carried out earlier. Perhaps there is a bang or scraping noise from beneath the car and the exhaust is loose or touching the road. Don't confuse these sounds with tools banging around inside the boot.

AFTER THE DRIVE: Having established that the bodywork is intact and mechanicals seem sound, or you think any repairs will be cheap to put right what you now need is a short breathing space. Getting an expert second opinion is vital. You will need time to organise this, so place a small 'holding deposit' and draw up a simple contract. See further in the BanGlossary. Make sure that the deposit is returnable subject to the car being inspected satisfactorily. Best not to talk about the amount you want to pay until the inspection is complete. If problems are found then that gives you the leverage to negotiate a better price or at least walk away from a problem car without making a huge loss and with a deposit back in your pocket. If the seller does not agree to this reasonable request then the car was probably not worth looking at in the first place.

NOTE: And if you are checking a future PTD (Personal Transportation Device) that runs on solar, steam or moral superiority power, the preceding few pages may be utterly irrelevant. However, it will still be the case that if there are leaks, strange smells, funny noises, unresponsive controls or something comes off in your hand, then you may well have a problem.

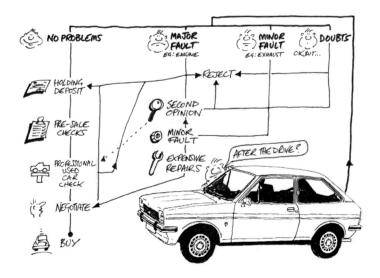

Bang Splutter Clang – Coursework

Eyes
Practise, practise and practise looking critically at all cars.
Look at your own car, a friend's and get out the clipboard.
Be critical.

Ears
Listen to cars that pass you in the street. Do they sound
healthy? What do you think the problem may be, if any?

Nose
Just be generally nosy about cars. Drive different ones
whenever you can. Take test drives whenever you can.

7

Banger Bona Fides

Getting it Checked

ALTHOUGH YOU HAVE GIVEN the car a once over to the best of your ability there are still some checks you can carry out and experts you can use to make absolutely sure that the car is in good condition and most importantly will actually belong to you. So is it safe, is it genuine? (That explains the pretentious bona fides title then.)

PREVIOUS OWNERS: If you want to be thorough and perhaps have a few doubts about the car, why not speak to the previous owner? This is especially useful if the owner had very recently sold it. Perhaps there was a problem. Their name and address would be on the registration document, so you should be able to look up their telephone number. Contact them at a reasonable hour, apologise for bothering them and ask for their help. Most of us like to be helpful and most owners are happy to either brag or cry about their old cars. Simply ask why they sold it, what was the condition like and what the mileage was when they sold it? Ask when the cam belt was last changed.

ROADWORTHINESS TEST: Some countries require this, but it is never a guarantee that a car is mechanically perfect. That is because it can easily develop a fault the day after the test and, believe it or not, some of these test documents are not entirely genuine. There are also many components that may not be checked and that can include the operation of something as important as the engine or gearbox. In most cases then you would be well advised to get the vehicle professionally checked.

GETTING IT CHECKED: Just as you would probably not buy a house without first paying for a professional survey it makes sense to do the same on a used car you want to buy. For many of us buying a car is very exciting and that means we can miss many faults. Indeed few of us have the expertise to distinguish a mechanically sound car from one which could cause us problems and expense in the future. So a report on a car's condition by an engineer is vital to avoid making a costly mistake. Having an inspection also means that you can negotiate a better price as faults can be pointed out to the seller and you can make a compromise on the price or insist that the seller fix any problems before you buy.

CHOOSE CAREFULLY: when picking an inspection company. Many of the leading national companies advertise in motoring publications and on websites. It is important to make contact with them and find out exactly what the costs are and what is included in the price. You also need to clarify whether the car you want to buy can be checked. Most companies aim to carry out the inspection within 72 hours, but some may be able to do it that day. Not every model or class of car can be checked. Some companies have restrictions on the types of vehicle that they will inspect. They may have age limitations, for instance over ten years old so won't look at a classic car. Commercial vehicles such as vans may be excluded and that also goes for imported vehicles. They could also have lists of exotic makes that they do not want to inspect.

WHAT IS CHECKED?: Inspection companies essentially provide a condition report on the car. They obviously cannot dismantle mechanical items or be expected to predict the potential life expectancy of the majority of components. Satellite navigation systems, anti theft devices and sound systems are usually not covered by the inspection because of their complexity. These items also have little bearing on how the car works. What they can spot though is faults that affect the performance of the car or its legality and any substandard mechanical or bodywork repairs. However, some companies may not inspect the interiors or report on cosmetic condition. Generally they will inspect the underside, bodywork and engine, then road test the vehicle.

HOW TO CHECK A CAM BELT: Unless you have X-Ray Specs you really can't check the condition without dismantling part of the engine. Essentially you have to rely on what the service history, if any, actually tells you. Most cars have cam belts, just a few have chains which don't break so easily. That is why in the service schedule there is a set mileage or period (say 3 years) for the belt to be replaced. If it is not changed eventually it will break and in 99 per cent of engines it will cause catastrophic damage. So all you have to go on is the service book, or possibly a receipt for the work done. That is as conclusive as it gets. If there is any doubt about when the belt was changed or according to the schedule it is due to be done, then you should get a quote from a garage for the procedure. Then if you buy the car either the seller agrees to have the change done, or the cost is deducted from the final asking price. However, if you do buy the car and there is any doubt at all about the service history then get it done. Cam belt lecture over.

COST: Although some companies have a flat fee system many will charge according to the engine size. You should ask what is included in this price as there may be warranties and also vehicle status checks to see if the car is stolen, an insurance write-off or still subject to a finance agreement.

AFTER THE CHECKS: You should get some form of written condition report either immediately after the inspection or within a few days. In many cases you can actually talk to the engineer carrying out the inspection, although this is not always possible. However, some companies may allow you to talk on the telephone to the inspector. Make sure that you clarify with the company exactly what you get in terms of access to the inspector and the details on the report. Once you have the report on the car you can start to make some decisions. Are there too many things to put right? Get quotes for repairs and on that basis you can decide what you are prepared to pay for the car.

ALTERNATIVELY: Rather than involve an inspection company you could just talk to your local garage. If you trust them and get on well, they should be more than happy to take a look at a car for you on their ramp, for perhaps an hour's labour, or if they really like you for free. It is unlikely they would offer a guarantee, but most important of all you would get their honest, professional opinion. You could even challenge the seller, if the car passes the professional inspection you pay and buy, if it doesn't you don't and renegotiate on what needs fixing. You will soon find out how confident the seller is about their car.

UNPLUGGED AGAIN?: A garage will happily hook a car up to an electronic diagnostic system but they will charge for this service. You may also be able to do this through a computer programme or possibly a mobile phone/handheld device. Technology in this area is being updated all the time. If it is an option use it.

STATUS or DATA CHECK: This involves the checking of various computer databases. In some countries it may be possible to find out whether the car is registered with the police as stolen, has ever been an insurance write-off or is still the subject of a finance agreement, plus other checks that confirm/deny the car is actually what it is advertised as. All these situations affect the ownership of a used car so it is vital that a status check is made. Other information may also be revealed when a status check is made including the last recorded mileage and any registration plate changes. This check can be made independently of any inspection and ideally having a data check first means that if it throws up any problems then there is no point having the vehicle inspected.

Banger Bona Fides – Coursework

Docs
Familiarise yourself with all the documents that come with a car so that you will know what's missing and what may be wrong. Ask to look at friends' and family's vehicle documents, you never know what you might spot!

Nurses
Contact the companies that offer inspection services and see which one offers you the service you want and will nurse you through the procedure.

8

Banger Banter

Doing the deal

EVERYTHING IS NEGOTIABLE AND there is every reason why you should try to make the asking price even friendlier. Negotiation is an art and can take years to learn, but there should be enough tips here to help you.

MAKE AN OFFER: Don't plough in too early with a price and delay talking about money for as long as possible. Let the seller invest time in you on the test drive and showing you around the car. Because only when you have examined the car and had it checked can you possibly say yes or no, and you should make the seller understand that this is the case. Maybe after going through the whole process including the test drive and professional inspection the seller will be desperate to get rid of you at any price!

Always bear in mind who you are negotiating with. A car dealer or trader is more versed in selling techniques, but they are not all high-pressure salesmen. Many have a take it or leave it attitude, itself an effective selling technique. Generally though, stick to the facts and don't be side tracked or distracted by offers of alternative cars, or deals. Don't be trapped into committing yourself when they ask 'if I could (do this, that or the other) will you buy the car?' Just stick to your original objectives of buying the best car you can afford. The advice is similar with the private seller, who might have more experience in the psychology of selling than you imagine. Again, stick to the car and the

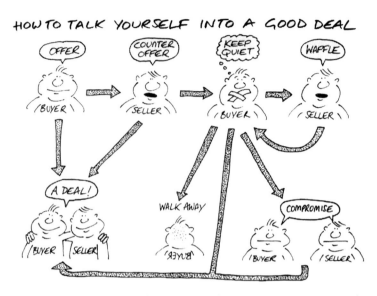

HOW TO TALK YOURSELF INTO A GOOD DEAL

plain facts and don't listen to sob stories. You are only interested in that car.

WHAT IS IN THE PRICE?: The first thing to establish is what is included in the price. This is the time to start reminding the seller of all the promises they made when you first met. The friend you should have taken with you to stop you making a mistake can also act as a human tape recorder. So establish for instance whether (where applicable) any road tax is included, or whether an item such as a tyre is to be replaced. With a dealer there are other issues, maybe they will service, and put a warranty on the car. With regards to the warranty read the terms carefully, ask the dealer what the cost would be without this cover and see if you can get the same or better protection elsewhere. **To sum up** if you don't like what is lumped in with the price, get it lumped out if it saves you money and it makes sense. A service would be a good thing, but make sure you get proof that this has been done before you collect the car.

WHAT TO OFFER: Of course your assessment of the car and the professional checks could have revealed some faults. Here you have a choice, either ask the seller to sort it out, or make an allowance in the price and get it fixed after you buy. For a selling dealer it will normally be a cheap or easy matter for them to deal with and to be honest, do you want the hassle? Now knock a bit off the price. How much is up to you. You are aware of the market by now. Think of a reasonable offer then knock a bit more off. Don't bid stupidly low, or upset the seller. By now you should have built up some sort of relationship and if you do get along then that will make the negotiations much easier. Remember to keep your humour and wits about you at all times and the supposedly stressful business of doing a deal will seem surprisingly easy.

DOING A DEAL: Simply say, *I'll pay £*_____ *for it.* Then stay quiet, don't justify it or hesitate, be straight and confident and then shut up. Babbling shows weakness. Ideally the seller will come back with a counter offer somewhere in the middle. You can counter again if the price seems high. Should the seller refuse to counter offer, or says no, or gives you the silent treatment then you say ... *Thank you for letting me see the car, goodbye.*
If the seller sincerely wants to do a deal they will stop you disappearing down the road and offer some sort of concession. If there is still room for compromise then consider it, but never go over your original offer. That is all there is to it, be patient, firm, but reasonable and always friendly and you should get your way.

PART EXCHANGE: Remember that other car in your life? The one that now seems in relatively good condition compared to the one you want to buy. Let's assume that you do not want the bother of selling it yourself. If you are prepared to part exchange it with a dealer bear in mind that they give the lowest possible figure they can. It will not be a near retail price that you could expect from a private sale, but a trade figure, which allows for any potential profit margin when it is resold. Once you understand that, then you are halfway to part exchanging your car. Usually what you want to agree then, is 'a figure to change' the net amount of money you will have to pay to get the other car.

My preferred technique is to only introduce your old car when the deal has been agreed, so that you effectively separate the two transactions. That puts the dealer on the defensive and unwilling to waste all their hard work and they may give you slightly more for your old car so that the whole transaction holds together. It is also likely that you will find out just what your car is worth.

Even before you start negotiating ideally you should contact dealers and anyone offering to buy vehicles so that you can quickly establish a rough trade price and know what the dealer is really offering. Understanding the trade value of your car is vital. Like any buyer, a dealer will respond well to a car that looks clean, tidy and well looked after, so at least give it a clean. Ideally though go to the chapter on selling your car (Bye Bye Banger) for more detailed advice on preparation and sell privately to maximise your money.

CONTRACT: Once you have thrashed out the deal now is the time to get it all down on paper. The details are relatively short and simple, all you need is a brief description of the car, the date, the price, if anything has been agreed to be rectified within that amount, the seller's name, address, and signature.

DEPOSITS: Although buying is essentially a case of paying and then driving (hopefully) into the sunset, there are circumstances when you may have to leave a little something as a deposit so that you can return later on. If there are a few things that the seller has agreed to sort out before collection leave a token amount of cash, keep the amount small and get a receipt. Note any sums paid and terms agreed to on the brief contract you draw up together and keep a copy. With dealers you should be able to leave an amount on a card. A credit card would give you some protection if there were a dispute.

INSURANCE: Turn back to the Head Bangers chapter, I trust you did research and took notes so that you can now arrange insurance cover. Here are some final reminders and tips: look at all the options and talk to lots of brokers, specialist car clubs and motor insurance companies. Shop around, but do not choose purely on price, the cover must be suitable to your motoring needs.

PAPERWORK: The registration document usually requires that both the buyer and seller sign or authorise the document and then the car can be re-registered in the buyer's name. You can find out up to date information easily and it is likely you will still be referred to as the New Keeper. Indeed, you might still get to keep a bit of the old registration document until the new one arrives to prove you are the owner. It is worth remembering that usually the seller remains liable for any offences committed until the registration authorities are informed of the change. So whatever you do make sure you grab any paperwork that you are entitled to including any service history or bills. Only then should you hand over the money.

PAYMENT: Traditionally the easiest way to pay is with cash. That may change and there may well be all sorts of excitingly secure ways of sending money. Ideally you want the one that costs the least as often you can be charged for sending larger amounts of money to others instantly. It sounds obvious, but only pay in full when you are actually taking the car, never, ever pay in advance.

COLLECTION: A favourite trick with less than honest sellers is to swop the half-decent mechanical parts for clapped out items. The new battery that helped to start the car first time could have been replaced by something that barely keeps its charge. Ditto the tyres – from street legal to bald penalty point items. So carefully look around for bits and pieces that look newer, or even older than before. Only then should you hand over the balance in either cash, or by banker's draft. Also remember to take a simple tool kit, consisting of some spanners and screwdrivers and possibly a jack if the car did not have one. A good idea could even be a gallon of fuel. Not surprisingly, many owners siphon off what remains in the tank, leaving you with little chance of reaching the local service station.

Banger Banter – Coursework

Talk Talk
Do a bit of negotiation with a friend. Ask them to pretend to sell and you pretend to buy. It could help sharpen your negotiation skills or lead to a ruddy big argument. What fun.

Double Talk
Need double glazing? Didn't think so, but why not make contact with some high-pressure sellers, not necessarily cars either and start negotiating. See if you can get your whole house reglazed for free. Don't invite them around or go through with a purchase, but this is still great practice.

9

Banged to Rights

The Legal Side

YOU ONLY GET WHAT you pay for, an annoying but accurate saying. It also follows that if you buy a heap, then it was your look out and your mistake. But if someone has misled, or tricked you in some way, why shouldn't there be a comeback? This brief legal guide assumes that the seller has not disappeared into thin air, but does not allow for the fact that the legal process can move no faster than the average snail. Let's assume that you have come to an embarrassing halt within minutes, or days, of purchasing your car. After slavishly following all the advice in this book, you might be thinking about going after the author. But think again, there are several legal options; the problem is though it can be very time consuming.

Obviously the law can change, a lot, but you can reckon that the general principles here are still going to apply for some time to come. Also the consumer law varies from country to country. So here are some very general, not country specific guidelines. Essentially if you buy privately you have far fewer rights than if you buy from a dealer. Simple. Buy private, sold as seen, or buy from a dealer and unless you agree otherwise you will have some comeback.

The guiding principle should be that you are trying to buy a cheap car and in most cases you should never expect too much. If the car goes wrong then put it down to experience. If you can sort something out with the seller amicably that would be far better for everyone. If you feel you have been done over and as a point of principle want to pursue the matter then that is up to you. In my experience, small claims are never worth the bother, especially if you are up against someone who routinely flouts the law.

However, let's look at the basic principles.

BUYING FROM A DEALER

In Europe anyway you have six months to complain about a fault. This means that car dealers and garages have to prove if they receive a complaint within six months about a car or part they supplied that it was perfectly useable when they sold it. That's right, the obligation is on them to prove it was in good condition.

In most parts of the world a car sold by a dealer must be of 'satisfactory quality', or of a standard that a reasonable person would regard as acceptable, bearing in mind the way it was described, how much it cost and any other relevant circumstances. This covers, for example, the appearance and finish of the car, its safety and its durability.

The car should also be 'free from defects', except when they were pointed out to you by the dealer, or is the sort of fault which should have been revealed by an inspection.

The car should also be 'as described' so a one-owner car must be just that. Fit for any normal purpose – so it must be a reasonably reliable car and capable of any tasks you specify such as seating seven passengers, or towing a caravan. So dealers must describe the car accurately and can't say that the car is a good runner if it isn't. Once you rely on a dealer's description it becomes a term of the contract, such as, 'It's definitely a 1998 model', whereas 'I think it's a 1998 model' would not be a term.

If you allow the dealer to put right the fault, however small, you have lost your right to reject the car. Alternatively you could allow the repairs, but put it in writing that you are accepting them 'Without prejudice' to your existing legal rights.

There may also be a civil action for breach of contract, if some term of the original agreement has not been met, e.g. a radio fitted, or delivery at a certain time. What you could get is a small amount of compensation. Alternatively, if the dealer is a member of a professional trade body, they may agree to abide by their conciliation and arbitration procedures. A dealer will also have to ensure that the car is roadworthy, unless it is sold specifically for parts, or breaking.

In addition to your legal rights, car dealers will be able to include a warranty. In some cases it could mean a comprehensive manufacturer backed warranty. All dealers offer some form of mechanical breakdown insurance ranging from 3 to 12 months although the terms and conditions have to be read very carefully, because there can be lots of exclusions.

BUYING PRIVATELY

It is worth repeating a paragraph from an earlier chapter 'Browsing for Bangers.' You could come across a decent, honest and helpful private seller with a perfect specimen to sell, or you could meet a rogue with a rough old car. You never can tell. The majority are honest, but may have bought an awful car without realising it, maybe they have lost all the service history, and possibly their advertisement misdescribes the car. Worst of all they think their car is worth a fortune. So if you thought buying from the motor trade is fraught with danger buying privately can often be much worse.

You have fewer rights if you buy privately. The seller must be legally entitled to sell the car, so obviously it must not be on finance, or stolen and only a data check will tell you this. The car must be as described by the seller. If a private seller lies about the condition of the car, you can sue for your losses, providing you can find the seller and want to go to the trouble of pursuing a claim through the civil courts. A private seller could get into trouble for selling a car that is not roadworthy.

SLOG THE BANGERNOMIC DOG, SAYS: **PRIVATE** SELLERS CAN GET AWAY WITH **MURDER!** HOWEVER, THEY CAN'T SELL AN UNROADWORTHY **BANGER. REMEMBER** IF A DEALER HAS POINTED OUT A FAULT, YOU CAN'T COMPLAIN ABOUT IT LATER. **LISTEN** CAREFULLY TO WHAT A SELLER SAYS ABOUT THE BANGER TAKE A **FRIEND**, THEY ARE USEFUL AS A WITNESS AND CAN **STOP** YOU MAKING AN **IMPULSE** PURCHASE. **PROMISES** MADE BY A DEALER MUST BE INCLUDED IN THE CONTRACT. FOR **PEACE OF MIND** BUY FROM AN ESTABLISHED DEALER, NOT ONE OPERATING IN A PHONE BOOTH.

Private or Trader? There is a huge amount of difference between a private seller against whom a buyer has virtually no redress and full time dealer who has all sorts of legal obligations to verify mileage and describe the car accurately. Obviously there can be a temptation for some traders to pretend to be private in order to dodge these responsibilities. The clues could be a seller with more than one car to sell and who wants to meet somewhere other than their premises. If their name is not on the registration document, then that is another big clue that they are buying cars to sell on.

Legal Action? In some cases, where only small amounts of money are concerned it certainly won't be worth your time and effort. Wherever you can, try and negotiate a settlement. In the case of a dealer most are reasonable and have a reputation to think of, so a letter to the owner, setting out your problems, politely and concisely, can produce the required results. However, if you think that the matter is serious, see a lawyer, though if the car was cheap there really is little point.

Generally there is an obligation on you to examine the car as far as it is reasonably possible, hence the phrase caveat emptor which means 'buyer beware'. Although you won't be expected to dismantle the gearbox, a visual inspection and test drive would be the minimal requirements. So buying blind and then claiming the car is rubbish is not usually an option. Also, if any defects are drawn to your attention then you are stuck with any faults.

Banged to Rights – Coursework

Avoid You don't really want to be involved in any legal dispute. It costs money and drags on longer than you would ever imagine. It is hassle to the power of several million, but it pays to be aware of what your rights are so wherever you live, check what your consumer rights are when you buy goods.

Decide This is your big decision, do you want some protection? Then buy from the trade, with a warranty. However, if you are more confident then buy private, it is as simple as that.

10

Bangers Under the Hammer

Buying at Auction

HERE IT IS, PERHAPS the most risky way to acquire a used car. Auctions will always exist in some form or other as they are one of the few ways, (subject to the reserve price) to guarantee the sale of a used car. Virtual Auctions (which you can view on a TV or computer screen) may take over and the same guidelines to buying online will apply (see p. 43, Browsing for Bangers). Although you can see photos and a live camera feed, you won't be able to drive the car. There is no substitute for actually seeing what you are going to buy, especially a car. So although you can click and buy, pay with a card and have the car delivered, here is the old fashioned way of buying at auction, which at least offers an interesting day out.

The point is that whether you buy privately, or from a car dealer it is unlikely that you will pay the lowest possible price. To stand a chance of doing that you need to visit an auction, but even then you could be gripped by bidding frenzy and pay more than it is worth. The other issue is things happen fast at auction, very fast indeed. If you miss one lot, another one will be along in a minute and then another and then another. Auctions are not for everyone. However, those who are prepared to do some research and use their common sense can buy a used car at a wholesale price. That is reason enough to consider making a bid at an auction, but before you do ...

The way auctions operate is very simple. Auctions are effectively the stock market of the used car industry. Vehicles are sold on behalf of the owners, who complete a legally binding form (the Entry Form), which attests to the vehicle's age, mileage and condition. Usually a reserve value is set, which is the lowest figure the seller will accept, so the auctioneers cannot sell below this value. Often the vehicles are grouped in categories, so there may be executive and prestige sales and nearly new cars. However, it is the general sales where just about any type of older vehicle can turn up, that we Bangernomics students love.

On the sale day itself all the vehicles should be lined up by lot order in their correct sale section ready to be sold and can be displayed under cover in well-lit viewing areas or outside. A printed or virtual sale catalogue should be available on the morning of the sale to help buyers around what looks like a massive car park. Before the sale starts there are a few hours for viewing. There may also be evening and weekend sales aimed more at the private buyer with cheaper cars although a larger number of buyers can actually increase prices.

So what happens? When the sale starts vehicles are driven into the auction hall usually in lot order. The car on sale stops in front of the rostrum and the auctioneer describes it to the buyers, a description that is

legally binding. They could be guaranteeing the mileage, mentioning any major mechanical faults, the existence of a service history, any warranties and whether there is a reserve price (although they obviously won't tell you what that is). Then the auctioneer will ask for a starting bid on the car. The bidding increments are controlled by the auctioneer reflecting the interest from the auction floor. Typically bidding is done in units of 5 or 10, starting at 10 and bigger 50 or 100 increments if the auctioneer thinks the crowd are enthusiastic. Don't worry about sneezing, or scratching your itchy nose. There are all sorts of apocryphal stories of people buying cars by mistake, but in today's professional market, that is never going to happen. Just bid clearly by raising your hand.

What cars go to Auction? Just in case you wondered, cars come from either the general public, dealers, company fleets, local authorities and finance companies. Dealers can dispose of cars because it is an unsuitable part exchange as it is too old, or just the wrong make. However, a large company may simply have a policy to auction cars over a certain age and mileage. Also the car could be too expensive to put right. Quite simply the car may have been stuck on their forecourt without finding a buyer and the dealer would rather have money in the bank than a depreciating hulk in the showroom. It is rare to find ordinary members of the public putting their cars through the auction. Again, there may be something wrong with the car, a problem that won't necessarily show up on its brief drive through the auction ring. That is why you need to be so very careful. Another group of vehicles are those classed as stolen/ recovered and sold by finance or insurance companies. Often they are damaged, but then they can also be in good condition. Other sources of auction fodder are fleet and company cars, which are usually no more than two, or three years old, often with a high mileage but backed up by a full service history. Vehicles can also come from large companies, or the public services such as the police and local authorities. These can lead a hard life but maintenance has usually been a priority so they may be scruffy with the remnants of a police decal peeling off the door, but still be a mechanically perfect vehicle.

Your first visit must always be your research trip. Leave all your money at home and just watch what goes on. It may frighten you off and for some that might be a good thing. Auctions aren't for nervous types. Get a copy of the Conditions of Sale and Entry  and any other information issued by the auctioneers. You will find out what rights you do and don't have especially as rules do vary between auction companies. Buy or download a price guide so that you can see what the vehicles are fetching compared to the printed prices. Always remember these price guides are just that, guides, and some models are more in demand than others. Also private buyers can push prices beyond what a dealer would be prepared to pay. Private repair costs will be far more

 compared to what some-one in the car trade would pay and this is always worth remembering. Condition is vital and ultimately a car at auction and anywhere else for that matter is only worth what someone is prepared to pay on the day and that could well be far too much.

Auction Language explained

Before the sale starts listen carefully to what the auctioneer says and also read any stickers on the car windows carefully.

'Without reserve' This means that the car will be sold to the highest bidder.

'Reserve' This is the minimum the seller will want for the car, not usually revealed before sale, unless it has been entered previously and didn't sell. Sometimes the auctioneer may give a clue to the reserve.

'As seen' What you see is what you get, including all the faults. Some cars fall into this category merely because of the seller's policy.

'All good', 'on description' or 'No major mechanical defects' This sounds promising, but it only applies to the major components, so although the engine, gearbox, axles, steering, suspension and brakes may be fine, instruments, electrics, tyres and trim may be broken or damaged. However, some auctions may offer an insurance backed warranty to cover this.

'Warranted all good' The auction actually guarantees that the car is as described with no major mechanical faults, with a warranted mileage and service history. A successful bidder can therefore reject a car if it is not up to these standards.

'Specified faults' A fault can be underplayed so a phrase such as 'worn gearbox' could actually mean that it is permanently stuck in second. It is worth bearing in mind that an auctioneer is acting as an agent for the seller and may only know as much about the car as they have been told.

Auction Survival Kit – what to take with you

Cash: The minimum amount required to pay a deposit although a card can be used, read the conditions of entry to find out how much.

Friend: To stop you making any rash bids, or buying something that you don't need. They can also drive you to the auction so you don't have to pay a delivery charge or make a return visit.

Old clothes: After all you will be crawling around getting a closer look won't you?

Torch: All the better to look into those nooks and crannies.

Magnet: When in doubt about filler rely on the old fridge magnet test.

Price guide: Printed or downloaded price guides do what they say.

Tool kit/gallon of fuel: to help you get the car you bid for home, but don't carry the petrol can around with you.

Before Bidding

Buy, take or download a sale catalogue. The cars will be parked together and on the windscreen will be a Lot Number. This gives some indication of the running order, but don't rely on it. There may also be some information about the car such as make, model, mileage and perhaps a brief engineer's assessment, which may not be binding anyway. Watch out for 'sold as seen' and 'recorded on insurance register' (that could mean it has been written off by an insurance company as a loss). Don't pin all your hopes on one Lot. It could be withdrawn, you might change your mind, or you might not bid enough to buy it, so draw up a shortlist of Lots.

Checking the car

There isn't much you can actually check. The cars are usually parked so close together it will restrict your view, most will be locked and they won't be started until a few minutes before being driven into the auction hall.

Entry form on windscreen. Read carefully for major faults, warranties and mileage.

Lot Number so you know roughly where it will appear in the sale.

Tyres for their condition tread and brand.

Bodywork look for rust, poor repairs and panel alignment.

Trim anything from a cracked windscreen to missing or damaged accessories.

Interior look for wear and tear, best done when the car is in the auction hall.

Engine are there oil leaks where it is parked? Be there when it is started so that you can check for smoke and listen for noises. The auction driver will usually let you look under the bonnet when it is in the auction hall.

How much to Bid?

Now is the time to set your budget. Look at the price guide trade price and bear in mind what similar vehicles made at the previous sales you attended. The questions are what can you afford and more importantly what are you prepared to pay? Obviously there is no point bidding up to what a main dealer would charge for a car with a year's warranty now is there? There may well be some local or national taxes to allow for. So listen carefully to what the auctioneer says about the Lot before they invite any bids.

Auction Action, a 10-point Bangernomic bidding plan

1. Before your Lot is called position yourself near the car you want. Use your friends if the Lots you are after are close together.
2. Watch the car being started. Does the oil light go and off quickly? Does it start first time? Does the engine sound healthy? Are there any strange noises? Is there thick black smoke from the exhaust? When the car moves off are there any creaks, groans or scraping sounds?

3. When driven to the auction hall it will join a short queue of cars. Now is your chance to take a good look inside. Maybe ask the driver to pop the bonnet. Make your decision now; do you want to bid for this car?

4. If you want to bid, place yourself in view of the auctioneer and listen. What they say now is crucial. Listen out for the good points like a warranty and guaranteed mileage and also any negative ones like 'gearbox trouble'.

5. Now programme yourself, what is your budget? And if you have a friend with you remind them to stop you bidding above that limit.

6. When the auctioneer suggests an opening bid and usually it is an optimistically high figure, don't get sucked in too early. Wait and see what happens.

7. When you bid, raise your arm clearly and confidently. Be aware of the margin of the bid: is it in 5, 10, 100, or more? If you want to make your bid less tell the auctioneer. Don't worry if the auctioneer ignores your bid because they usually concentrate only on two bids at a time.

8. If you seem to be bidding against someone you can't see, it is permissible for the auctioneer, subject to their company rules, to take 'bids off the wall'. They do this to get closer to the reserve price. So don't get carried away and exceed your bidding budget.

9. If you drop out of the bidding a shake of the head is sufficient to indicate this to the auctioneer.

10. If your bid is successful you will be required to pay an immediate deposit, usually 10% or a fixed sum in cash.

After the sale

The balance will need to be paid within a short period, usually 24 hours, or sometimes before the auction closes, by cash, or credit/debit card. You may also have to pay an indemnity fee on a sliding scale according to the cost of the vehicle which insures you against the car being stolen, an insurance write-off, or still on finance. You may also have to pay a buyer's fee which is a percentage of the final hammer price. Bear in mind that if you delay in paying the full amount you will probably be charged storage fees, so don't delay.

If your bid is successful but it does not exceed the reserve figure set by the seller, then the auctioneers will contact them to find out if they will accept less. In the meantime don't bid for another car or you might end up with two! Should the seller make a counter offer the decision is yours, but don't exceed your budget, or pay more than you think it is actually worth.

If you have bought a vehicle that came with a trial, in most cases you will only have one hour after payment to drive the car and find a serious fault. If a car is sold on an independent engineer's report (attached to the windscreen), or 'with no major mechanical faults' then that is exactly how you should expect the car to be. Remember that it is up to you to check the car's overall exterior visible

AUCTION CHECK

Ⓐ **TYRES**: CHECK CONDITION/TREAD
Ⓑ **ENTRY FORM**: READ CAREFULLY. IT DETAILS MOT, MAJOR FAULTS, WARRANTIES AND MILEAGE.
Ⓒ **LOT NUMBER**: MAKE A NOTE SO THAT YOU KNOW WHEN IT WILL APPEAR IN THE SALE.
Ⓓ **BODYWORK**: LOOK FOR MAJOR RUST, POOR REPAIRS, BAD PAINTWORK, PANEL ALIGNMENT.
Ⓔ **TRIM**: CRACKED WINDSCREEN, MISSING OR DAMAGED ACCESSORIES.
Ⓕ **INTERIOR**: DAMAGE, ESPECIALLY DASHBOARD AND SEATS. OPEN DOOR WHEN IT GOES INTO SALE.
Ⓖ **ENGINE**: OIL LEAKS WHERE PARKED. BE THERE WHEN CAR IS STARTED. LOOK FOR SMOKE, LISTEN FOR NOISE. RAISE BONNET IN SALE.

condition – paintwork, trim, tyres and the interior, seats and carpets – for example – prior to sale. Never forget the phrase, 'sold as seen'.

Collection

Once you have paid, the office should be able to give you all the relevant paperwork including service history and registration document, plus a sound system front, or anything else removed from the vehicle for security reasons. You will also get a pass out form allowing you to take the car off the premises. If the registration is missing, the auctioneer's receipt is sufficient proof of ownership until you can apply for a replacement.

Before you drive off though make sure that your insurer will cover you. Also remember that the vehicle has to be roadworthy so one balding tyre or dodgy wiper blade would be illegal and ought to be fixed. It is not unknown for police to park outside the auction exit and target illegal vehicles.

When you get the car home sort out any problems and unless there is any evidence that it has been done recently, have the car serviced.

Bangers Under the Hammer – Coursework

Walk The best way to learn about an auction and find out if you are comfortable with the whole experience is to go to as many as possible. Don't bid, don't take any money just look and learn.

Write down prices. Compare and contrast with the prices in classified ads. They might not be too much different. Look at the condition of the cars at the auction. Would you really buy or at least bid for one?

11

Banging About

Banger 'Care'

YOU HAVE SAFELY STEERED your banger home, it is taxed, insured and possibly freshly serviced. What next? Well you could give it a clean. Bangernomics students can now divide themselves into two categories. Leave it as you found it, or beautify and personalise. At the very least you ought to get rid of the more disgusting leftovers belonging to the previous owner, banana skins, crisp packets and old passengers that seem reluctant to leave. This can be done quickly, easily and without resorting to expensive specialist 'products'.

BODYWORK: All you need is some hot water and a sponge to get rid of the grime. If you have some car shampoo use it. Rinse off the suds with some clean water and that is it. I

won't go over the top with precise washing and waxing tips, but now might be a good time to check inside for water leaks, usually through broken window rubbers.

ENGINE: Resist the temptation to clean under the bonnet. Water and engines don't mix, they have a habit of refusing to start, or suddenly developing intermittent electrical faults. What you can do though, is wipe the grease off the items that you will need to check periodically. Use a rag lightly dipped in petrol. If the car has not recently been serviced to your knowledge, then a simple oil change will help. Don't forget the cam belt change if the engine needs it.

WINDOWS: For your own safety, you ought to be able to see out. The traditional household window cleaners aren't really suitable for cars as they polish the glass and leave a reflective glare. The biggest problem, even after the glass has been washed, is the presence of grease, which smears all over the windscreen. The simple answer is to use the pages of a newspaper which will soak up the grease. Also rub the paper over the wiper blades to prevent the grease returning.

INTERIOR: A good old-fashioned dustpan and brush, or vacuum cleaner, will do the job. If any of the carpets or mats can be detached from the floor, get them out. Domestic furniture polish will do if you want to buff up plastic seats and dashboards, otherwise a damp cloth will soak up the worst of the dust. If there are some persistent smells, or festering stains, don't be frightened to use well-known brands of disinfectant.

BANGER MECHANICS: If it isn't broken, don't even attempt to fix it. This has to be the Bangernomics watchword when it comes to fiddling about with anything mechanical. Once you start interfering, the fine balance of the car is disturbed and things will start to go wrong, even if you know what you are doing. Some Bangernomics students may care to regard the bonnet as a sealed unit, and simply rely on the experts when trouble strikes. That is one way of approaching it, but of course prevention is always better than costly cure. So a minimum of maintenance and observation should keep everything running smoothly especially if you want to avoid coming to an embarrassing halt.

Cars have certainly become a lot more complicated and DIY isn't always an option. The fact is that the view under the bonnet is either dauntingly complicated or it actually looks like a sealed unit because there are big, dumb plastic covers. This depressing sight is only relieved by playful yellow screw tops that we are allowed to touch. But never mind all that, here is a brief mechanical numbskull's guide to keeping the cogs turning on cars with conventional petrol and diesel engines. For anything else the general principles for looking after these new fangled PTDs (Personal Transportation Devices) are going to be similar. However, paying attention to what the owner's manual says, being methodical about certain procedures and finding a local servicing agent, or expert is still important. So I'd still read this even if your transportation device hovers.

WORKSHOP MANUAL: This will save many frustrating hours searching for various items and deciding which spare part is right for the car. They can help you trace a simple fault and are invaluable for telling you how to take bits off properly. These can often be picked up for older cars second-hand. Otherwise there is always the local library. If you can't find or borrow one I would argue that however complicated cars are these days even buying a brand new manual is a worthwhile investment. You'll be amazed at how satisfying it is to repair something simple like a windscreen washer and the detail in the book at least mean you will be poking at the right piece of kit. Compared to what a garage may charge for sorting that problem out the book will easily pay for itself.

OIL: At the very least the first thing you should do is change the oil unless you have proof (receipts) that it has been done recently. In simple terms the oil provides lubrication. When it gets old and black, with bits of metal in it, then the liquid is less effective and starts to damage the engine. So changing the oil and oil filter is a good place to start and in most cases finish. If you don't want to get your hands dirty, ask someone else to do it. The more enthusiastic can perform this simple service by referring to the manual.

JOIN THE CLUB: If there is a national, or local club for your car or marque it could well be worth taking out a membership. Often they negotiate discounts on insurance and other motoring services plus more importantly they have a huge amount of specialist knowledge. If you have a technical problem they can usually make a useful suggestion. Some also have a thriving parts service and find items that are impossible to source elsewhere.

RESCUE/RECOVERY SERVICE: Although the cost of joining might even in some cases exceed the value of your banger, it is essential to invest in this service, especially if you plan to rely on the car. The only exception might be if you restrict the car's adventures to local runs. These days it is a very competitive market and there are some very low membership costs for a basic rescue/recovery service. However some companies may charge more for older vehicles, or ones they believe to be less reliable so always shop around and look at the small print. As with any service try to compare like with like.

TOOL KIT: A motley collection of spanners and screwdrivers are all you really need. Adjustable spanners make sense, although the purist mechanic won't be impressed. The only specialist tool would be a spark plug spanner. Self-locking grips, sometimes referred to as a 'Monkey Wrench' can prove useful. A collection of screwdrivers both with a flat and cross heads is a good idea. Also a proper wheel brace is worth having as sometimes the pathetically small spanners supplied with the car have little or no chance of removing the wheel nuts. Other items include: fuel can; cloth; adhesive tape; spare bulbs and fuses; tyre pressure gauge; foot pump; battery charger; and jump leads. Buy good quality items and they will last for the length of your Bangernomic career. Oh yes and stick them in an old bag, there is no point having them rattling around in your boot which will just annoy everyone. And finally put some old clothes in the bag. If there is something you can fix easily you won't want to get your decent clothing dirty. However stupid you look in an old pair of trousers and jacket they will keep the worst of the dirt away.

WARRANTY: This is essentially an insurance policy which covers your car against specific mechanical failures. Not everyone bothers but maybe they should because on some cars it is certainly worthwhile because they are so pricey to fix. You can even get a policy which covers maintenance and effectively spreads any servicing and repair costs over the year. It will suit some drivers perfectly and remove any worries they have about unexpected expenditure. To get the best warranty that suits you it is important to read the small print to see exactly what is covered. You may have a claims limit and be required to contribute to any costs. Indeed high mileage vehicles and older Bangers may not be eligible for cover at all.

ADVANCED TOOL KIT: If you do take DIY car maintenance much more seriously and intend to do a lot of work yourself then I'll assume you know what you need, however I would like to issue a little health and safety notice at this point.

HEALTH & SAFETY MESSAGE: It is never properly comfortable underneath any car and the only truly safe way to work is using a professional two or four post hoist that you can find in a garage, or failing that an inspection pit. In both those situations the chances of being injured by the car falling on your head are very remote. Unfortunately many home mechanics are damaged because they do not take the right precautions. Bricks, timber, and breezeblocks are all inappropriate ways of balancing a car in the air. Also a jack should not be the sole item keeping a car airborne whilst you work underneath. Indeed the scissor type jacks supplied with most cars are only intended for use when quickly changing a wheel. If you intend to regularly work underneath a car you need the right equipment, this means an hydraulic jack. However you must use the equipment properly because the approved jacking points adjacent to wheels are really only suitable for changing wheels. Hydraulic jacks should only be positioned on suspension cross members, or on rear wheel drive cars the differential. Never locate the jack on the engine sump or floor. Once raised then axle stands should be used to support the car. Even so, many mechanics still do not feel completely safe when a car is on axle stands as some cars could still be pushed off by someone leaning on the car. Ramps can also make sense, but ideally you should only put a car on them with help and the wheels need to be chocked properly (put something heavy behind wheels) to stop the car and the ramps moving. Yes there is more to getting a car up into the air than you imagined. If you have any doubts don't do it and always consult the manufacturer about the positioning of axle stands and hydraulic jacks.

There is lots of other safety stuff too, like don't smoke when you are looking into the fuel tank and don't change the oil when naked, that sort of thing. I reckon you have enough common sense to decide what's right and what's wrong. Just be sensible, don't take any unnecessary risks and you won't hurt yourself. If you don't have the skills then ...

DON'T TAMPER WITH: brakes, suspension, or steering. For the enthusiastic, though incompetent, apprentice mechanic, steer clear of fiddling with parts that could endanger your health and other people's lives.

ROUTINE SERVICING: Get it serviced. Either you do it, or get someone who is qualified to do it, this is vital to keeping your banger healthy. Service intervals vary from car to car, so an inspection could occur at between 1,500 to 3,000 miles for older classics through to 12,000 for more modern cars, whilst some state of the art cars only require a 20,000 mile or more check. Everything depends on the vehicle's age and the type of engine. You will find details of what is involved at each interval in the workshop manual or owner's handbook. Even if you only cover a tiny mileage annually, you should still have a service at least once a year, otherwise minor faults may develop into major problems.

YOUR LOCAL GARAGE: Your best friend when it comes to keeping a car in tip top condition is more than likely to be your local garage. If you go to a main agent with plate glass and pot plants then you are going to be paying for all that. A small independent local garage will have a much lower hourly labour rate. It isn't just about money of course, you need to establish that the garage is a good one. You can only find that out by asking around friends and neighbours. Personal recommendation is best, but I also feel that a bad local garage will soon get found out. It is in their interests to deal with their customers honestly and fairly otherwise they will run out of business. I have found that a good garage won't do any unnecessary work and will do their best to solve problems economically. When in doubt though make contact with your local trading standards office or local equivalent to see if there have been a series of complaints against the garage. Also membership of a garage association should mean that there are complaints procedures and certain standards required for membership. This is still not a guarantee that you will be happy with the garage. Essentially you need to get on with them and they need to understand what you want and what you can afford. A good garage will never do work without consulting you first. Spending time finding the right mechanic is just as important as finding the right Banger.

BANGERNOMICS GOOD GARAGE GUIDE: As well as local recommendation, why not join a car club specific to your car? Most have recommended garages that as well as being experts in particular models may offer discounts on parts and servicing to members.

Once you have found your garage you then need to set your own agenda and be aware of the costs involved. Money seems to be at the root of a lot of service related problems. Calculating the cost of work is not difficult. There are manufacturer standard times for all procedures, whether it is unscrewing a bolt, or a major crash repair. Just call the manufacturer to find out these times and then all you need to know is the garage's labour charge. This charge obviously varies depending on their location. Multiply the figures and not only can you check their sums when you have the bill, once you have a figure you can now shop around for a better quote. Getting a full quote should alert you to the worst of the bad practices such as charging for oil by the litre and being charged under sundries for the mechanic's rubber gloves.

Ensure that any local taxes and parts costs are included otherwise there will be a nasty surprise. Always remember to put what you want done in writing, state a collection time and the minimum you agree to spend. This saves a lot of confusion and expense later. Most importantly make it clear that you will authorise any additional work. It is not uncommon to be presented with a big bill and a new engine simply because you insisted on the car being ready by 5pm. When it comes to the 'can't get the parts' excuse, most garages have standard service items in stock, but the majority of parts can be delivered within 24 hours. Oh yes and once the car has been fixed you can ask to see the parts that have been replaced.

If you do have service and repair related problems, talk to the service or garage manager straight away. If the problem cannot be resolved, you will still have to pay the disputed bill to get your car back. However, give the garage a letter, detailing your complaint, saying that you are dissatisfied and that payment is made 'without prejudice' to your legal rights. This will ensure that the garage cannot say in court (if it ever gets that far) that you accepted the repair because you paid the bill. So here is what you need to do to get a good garage and good service.

- Ask friends/relatives for recommendations.
- Are they members of a professional body?
- Ask manufacturer for repair times and what is actually serviced.
- Tell garage in writing what you want done.
- Check whether costs for labour, parts and taxes are all included.
- Ask if workmanship and parts are guaranteed.
- Get quotes and second opinions from other garages.

- Request that you are consulted about any additional work/expenditure.
- Agree collection and payment arrangements.
- Get a detailed invoice showing a breakdown of all parts/labour costs.

GARAGE CHAINS: Rather than being a family owned garage there are a number of nationwide chains, sometimes called fast fit centres with lots of bays and ramps and the promise of fixing your car for less. This is not always the case. It is vital to compare prices as often a local garage can match or beat a quote. However, these chains may be best for supplying and fitting some consumables, like tyres and exhausts.

WEEKLY CHECKS: What you have to do is get into some sort of routine. Put aside fifteen minutes on the weekend just to carry out these simple checks. It means you will be able to quickly spot any deviations from the norm, so that you can trace any fault and most importantly get it fixed. The following are general recommendations and are no substitute for consulting an expert mechanic, which you must always do when in any doubt. Also many cars have diagnostic systems and could very smugly tell you what is wrong. However, the sensors located at various parts of the car can become corroded and dirty, so are not completely reliable.

OIL: According to the experts you should check your oil level at least every 500 miles or once a week. And at the risk of sounding patronising you should place the car on level ground. Drives and roads can have inclines and many drivers just don't allow for this. I'll assume you know what the dipstick looks like. On older cars it will be sited in the middle of the engine. Modern cars have a bright yellow cap. Take it out, wipe it off and feed it in again. Take it out and

THE ⑩ POINT ⑮ MINUTE BANGERNOMIC WEEKLY CHECK ►

OIL	HYDRAULIC FLUID	WATER	WIPERS / WASHERS	TYRES
BATTERY	FANBELT	HOSES	LIGHTS	NOISES

now read it. This is necessary; as it's likely some oil will creep along the gauge when the engine is shut off so the first measurement will be wrong. On most vehicles there are two marks on the gauge. The oil level must be between the upper and lower marking. You will find in your owner's manual how much oil you must add for topping up. Generally this will be between 0.5 and 1 litre. Don't be in a hurry, just add a little at a time and return after five to ten minutes to check the level. You must consult the manual or the manufacturer for the definitive procedure because although the engine should be switched off for the majority of cars there are some exceptions. When you add oil it is a good idea to have a clean rag ready so that you can wipe around the cap so that any dirt doesn't get inside the engine, then keep it nearby to mop up spills. It sounds obvious, but you should never overfill an engine. That's because seals may start to leak, also the oil can foam which can push oil into areas where it is not supposed to be. And finally always use the correct oil and grade. The owner's manual or the car's manufacturer will be able to tell you what that will be.

Problem: Noticeable increase in oil consumption when checking level and patches of oil when parked.
Cause: Engine oil leaks.
Solution: Depends on where leak is; when new gaskets or seals are required then this is a garage job.
Problem: Increased oil consumption and noticeable blue smoke from the exhaust.
Cause: Worn engine is burning oil.
Solution: Garage may need to fit new valve guide seals, or more seriously new pistons and rings, maybe a new engine. Oh no!

HYDRAULIC FLUID: Both the clutch and brakes rely on specialised fluid to keep them working. Sometimes they are located in plastic bottles and at other times metal pots towards the back of the engine compartment. Refer to your manual for the correct levels. Only a tiny amount of fluid is necessary to maintain the correct level. Do not allow the level to drop as air could enter the system and seriously affect their efficiency. Be careful when handling the fluid, as it is highly corrosive both to paintwork and skin. If you need to top up then unscrew the cap, remove it carefully and place it on a piece of clean cloth. Top up to the max mark and use a good quality fluid.

Problem: Brake fluid level drops rapidly.
Cause: Leak in system.
Solution: Don't drive the car and consult a garage.

POWER STEERING FLUID: Check where the fluid reservoir is in your owner's manual or service book. If you need to remove the filler cap, wipe around it and then remove.

Some may have hot or cold level markings and depending on the temperature ideally the fluid should be at that level. If it needs to be topped up, make sure you use the correct brand and type of fluid. Don't overfill and screw the filler cap on tightly.

Problem: Fluid level drops.
Cause: Possible leak in system.
Solution: Get it checked at a garage.

BELTS: One or more of these usually runs around several pulleys (such as crankshaft, alternator and fan) and probably will be connected to other engine parts such as air conditioning, power steering and water pumps. They should be at the correct tension so that they either don't slip, or aren't on so tight that they strain the components. Push and pull the belt where it has the longest connection, the movement should be no more than 5 to 10mm. For adjustment, consult the manual, but the usual method is to slacken the bolts on the alternator and move it until the tension is correct. Now look at the belt for signs of fraying or cracks, any shiny areas are bad, as are splits. If you have any doubts about the condition of belt (which normally lasts about two years) then replace it immediately.

Problem: Screech or squeal.
Problem: The belt may be too slack.
Solution: Tighten.
Problem: Constant hum at idle or when pulling away.
Problem: The belt may be too tight.
Solution: Slacken.

COOLANT: Some cars have sealed cooling systems, which do not require regular attention, but it is always worth checking the water level, as you don't want to overheat. Never check when the engine is hot and, if warm, use a cloth to remove the radiator cap. Refer to manual, but usually the water must be visible and covering a level mark. Plastic expansion tanks are also common and will usually be marked high and low on the side. This is also a good time to check for anti-freeze especially if it is getting towards winter. If there are no greenish traces, buy some from an accessory shop and follow the instructions. Consult the manufacturer's handbook on this one because cars now have sealed for life systems or must use certain brands or types of fluid.

Problem: Water level drops rapidly.
Cause: Leaks from hoses, possibly radiator.
Solution: Replace hoses, fit, or repair radiator. Radiator additives to stop leaks are available from accessory shops.
Problem: Water loss, but also noticeable overheating when the temperature gauge indicates high or is in the red.
Cause/Solution: If there are squeaks and leaks from the water pump then that may need replacing. The radiator could be blocked, or leaking, then stop the leak with additive, clean, or replace.

BATTERY: Most batteries are now sealed and there is no need to check the water levels. There could be a condition indicator and you may need to consult the handbook or instructions on how to read it. However some older and classic car batteries require you to check the levels, keeping the water just above the tops of the cells. Use tap water, or distilled water which can bought from accessory shops. Check the terminal connections for tightness and clean away any corrosion either with a brush, or just warm water. A layer of Vaseline around the terminal posts will keep the white corrosion deposits away. Do not forget to check the security of the battery, which may be held in position with a strap. If it falls over, it could start a fire and cause considerable damage to the surrounding area from spilled acid.

Problem: Battery levels drop rapidly.

Cause: Charging rate high, or the battery plates are faulty, or a cell could be leaking due to a crack in the casing.

Solution: In most cases the battery is due for replacement. Talk to a specialist if in doubt, though some leaks can be repaired with a special filler.

Problem: Sluggish starting. If headlights dim or go out when starting.

Cause: Battery may be nearing the end of its life and not holding its charge.

Solution: Use a test meter, or a battery charger with a display to see what the condition is. Usually the reading should be above 12 volts, because at 12 or below the battery may be flat. If you only do short journeys this is not good for a battery which may need more regular charges.

HOSES: Check the ones attached to the radiator, the top hose is the easiest to see. Are there any obvious water leaks, especially from each end? If so, are the clips holding it in place tight enough? Use a screwdriver. Are there any cracks or splits? Now squeeze it, if lots of cracks appear or the rubber feels very soft then it must be replaced. Usually this is a simple job and will save you much grief. Look also at the rubber pipes, which connect to the heater, or air conditioning system, which should also be in good condition.

Problem: Water level drops rapidly.

Cause: Leaks from hoses.

Solution: Replace hoses, or repair radiator.

Problem: Water loss, but also noticeable overheating when the temperature gauge is high.

Cause/Solution: If the ignition light stays on then the fan belt needs replacing.

SCREENWASH: Usually the plastic screenwash container is fairly obvious either to one side or rear of the engine bay.

You can simply top up with tap water although sometimes that can be a little harsh and contain lime scale. If you really care use filtered or softer rainwater. Whatever you do though put a proper additive in, (not washing up fluid) which will de-ice and help clean the screen. Some cars have one container others may have separate ones for headlamp and even rear washers. When filling up wipe away dirt from around the filler neck, then pull off cap.

Problem: Falling level even when screenwash not being used.
Cause/Solution: Possible split in container or in pipes. Replace broken item.
Problem: Blocked washer jet.
Solution: unblock with a pin.

WIPERS: Look at the blades, they must not be perished or frayed. Ideally give them a clean as detailed before, but you can also clean the edge of the blade with a cloth dipped in screenwash.

Problem: Areas are left unwiped, with oily streaks which restrict view.
Cause: Windscreen wipers are perishing and may not be making proper contact with the window due the mechanism being worn. Dirty windscreen.
Solution: Replace windscreen wipers and add special screen-wash to the washer bottle.

TYRES: Check their pressures ideally with a pencil type gauge, which you push into the tyre valve. Take readings when the tyres are cool, otherwise the pressure increases and gives a false reading. If you overfill release air by pressing loosely against the valve. Use either a foot pump, or forecourt inflator (which usually has to be paid for). You should also look at the car's handbook (sometimes inside of fuel flap) for the definitive information on tyre pressures front and rear and variations when there are just two passengers as opposed to five. Also check the condition of the tyres for wear, cuts in the tread or sidewalls, bulges in the sidewalls and stones or foreign objects trapped in the tread grooves, which should be removed. It is also useful to check for leaks from the valves, especially following inflation, and to replace missing valve caps. Don't forget to check the spare (if fitted) too.

Problem: Tyre pressure dropping.
Cause: Leak or slow puncture.
Solution: Consult tyre specialist as it may be beyond repair. Always get a second opinion if the fault is not obvious enough to you.
Problem: Uneven tyre wear, especially on the front wheels.
Cause: Misaligned brakes, or damaged suspension.
Solution: May simply need the tracking corrected, which is a cheap, and simple garage job. Could be suspension, which is more dangerous, consult a garage.
Problem: Worn centre section of tyre.
Cause: Over inflation.
Solution: Correct pressure.

LIGHTS: Don't wait for a car's warning light system to tell you that something may not be working. They aren't always accurate anyway. An incredible amount of muck is thrown up from the road, which then clings to the light lenses. This means other drivers won't see you and in turn you may not be able to see where you are going. So simply wipe them over with a damp cloth or sponge. Periodically check that all the lights work with a friend doing the honours on the outside. Alternatively, if you haven't got any friends then the reflections from shop windows can provide an instant check.

Problem: Indicators flash faster than normal on one side of the car.

Cause: A bulb has blown or one that is the incorrect wattage has been fitted. Consult your manual.

Problem: Indicators flash very slowly.

Cause: Incorrect bulb, faulty electrical circuit, faulty flasher unit.

Solution: Replace bulb or indicator unit, or clean up terminals, see below.

Problem: No indicators.

Cause: Blown Fuse. Wiring Fault. Indicator switch broken. Flasher unit broken.

Solution: Replace units, but essentially you may need the whole circuit checked.

Problem: Light does not work, or only works intermittently.

Cause: Bulb may have blown. Look at the wire element inside the bulb. Otherwise look at the connections for any corrosion.

Solution: Clean connections and use a water dispersant (WD40). Look at wires for security and check the earth wire, which connects to the bodywork, is tight and not corroded. Clean, use sandpaper and water dispersant.

ELECTRICAL FAILURE: If something doesn't work (radio, windscreen wipers) then more than likely a fuse will have blown. Replacing them is easy. Refer to the manual to locate the fuse box and simply pull out and replace with one that has an identical rating. If it blows again then there is a problem with the electrical circuit or the item itself.

CLEANING: Something you ought to do at least every few weeks or months. It means that you get to examine the bodywork closely and can spot any problems, faults, or leaks more quickly.

DURING THE WEEK: Simply make a mental note during your weekly motoring trips of any strange noises, or driving characteristics. If the brakes are less effective or the engine is sluggish then you will need to get that inspected. Refer back to the BANG, SPLUTTER, CLANG chapter, or consult your local garage to identify the problems.

REPLACEMENT PARTS

You really do need to think Bangernomically and that means not taking the simple option when it comes to parts. You could just visit a nearby main dealer, who may well be the cheapest and possibly the only supplier. However that is doubtful and many manufacturers end up deleting certain items from their stocks eventually. So you will have to resort to alternative sources and with the global market-place you could end up buying from a private seller, a specialist parts supplier, an owner's club or a dealer on the other side of the world.

Body Panels: These can be bought second hand and cleaned from a salvage or scrap yard. There are also 'Pattern Parts', effectively low priced copies which are actually more difficult to fit sometimes, but perfectly adequate.

Engine/Gearbox: The oily parts of a car are usually terrifically expensive when bought new. However, there are companies which recondition these parts. You give them your worn out bits and they exchange them for one they prepared earlier.

Interior: Pieces of trim and even seats can be expensive and impossible to find, so it is always best to go to a salvage yard first. Owners' clubs are also great places for these sorts of obscure items.

Banging About on a Shoestring

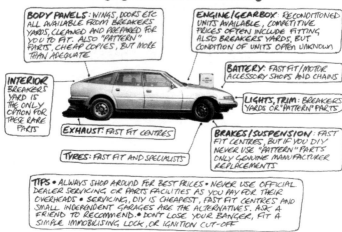

BODY PANELS: WINGS, DOORS ETC. ALL AVAILABLE FROM BREAKERS YARDS, CLEANED AND PREPARED FOR YOU TO FIT. ALSO "PATTERN" PARTS, CHEAP COPIES, BUT MORE THAN ADEQUATE

ENGINE/GEARBOX: RECONDITIONED UNITS AVAILABLE., COMPETITIVE PRICES OFTEN INCLUDE FITTING ALSO BREAKERS YARDS, BUT CONDITION OF UNITS OFTEN UNKNOWN

INTERIOR BREAKERS YARD IS THE ONLY OPTION FOR THESE RARE PARTS

BATTERY: FAST FIT/MOTOR ACCESSORY SHOPS AND CHAINS

LIGHTS, TRIM: BREAKERS YARDS OR "PATTERN" PARTS

EXHAUST: FAST FIT CENTRES

BRAKES/SUSPENSION: FAST FIT CENTRES, BUT IF YOU DIY NEVER USE "PATTERN" PARTS ONLY GENUINE MANUFACTURER REPLACEMENTS

TYRES: FAST FIT AND SPECIALISTS

TIPS • ALWAYS SHOP AROUND FOR BEST PRICES • NEVER USE OFFICIAL DEALER SERVICING OR PARTS FACILITIES AS YOU PAY FOR THEIR OVERHEADS • SERVICING, DIY IS CHEAPEST, FAST FIT CENTRES AND SMALL INDEPENDENT GARAGES ARE THE ALTERNATIVES. ASK A FRIEND TO RECOMMEND. • DON'T LOSE YOUR BANGER, FIT A SIMPLE IMMOBILISING LOCK, OR IGNITION CUT-OFF

Banging About – Coursework

Just Keep on Banging on and on and on . . .

Your coursework is simply keeping up with the maintenance schedules. If you have never done this before or you have not bought your Banger yet then practise on someone else's car. Ask if you can look after it for week. You never know you might save a fortune by tipping them off about an impending problem. Now that really will impress them.

SLOG THE **BANGERNOMIC** DOG WOULD LIKE TO REMIND YOU THAT **CLEANLINESS** IS NEXT TO **GODLINESS.** LOOK AFTER YOUR **BANGER** AND IT WILL LOOK AFTER YOU. WEEKLY CHECKS OF THE TYRES, OIL AND WATER ETC **REDUCES** YOUR CHANCES OF **BREAKING DOWN.** CLEANING THE WINDOWS AND LIGHTS MEANS THAT YOU CAN SEE AND BE SEEN. KEEPING YOUR **BANGER** HEALTHY IS VITAL AS THE **MOT** GETS TOUGHER. **NEVER** COMPROMISE ON MAINTAINENCE. A **BANGER** CAN BE RUN **COST EFFECTIVELY** BUT IF YOU CAN ONLY AFFORD TO ADD PETROL **TAKE THE BUS**

12

Bye Bye Banger

Banger disposal

WHEN TO SELL YOUR car is one of life's great imponderables. The exception is when a mechanic shakes his head and the garage quotes an eye-watering sum for helping it to limp through another year. Alternatively you might need a different kind of car, one that's bigger, smaller, faster, or more frugal. As you must have gathered by now Bangernomics shows you how to buy and run a car cost effectively, so to make this a comprehensive guide to selling as well, would mean that the book would be twice as thick and twice the price. However, turning your car into cash is a very important principle of Bangernomics. So when should you consider selling your Banger?

Condition: The best time to sell is before the car needs major repairs, so pass the crystal ball. By now you might be able to recognise the tell tale sounds of expensive repairs. The principle is the same as when buying, serious body repairs are costly, whilst mechanical items can usually be simply replaced. A reconditioned engine may well be cheaper than the hassle of selling the car you have and buying a replacement, which will be an unknown quantity.

Time: Buying and selling cars is largely a seasonal activity, see the Head Bangers chapter for details. Obviously the right car at the right price will always find a buyer, but generally, don't sell in mid-winter, or after the spring and autumn new car rush when there are lots of used vehicles about. In high summer everyone is on holiday and you may not get a good response to your advertisement whereas spring is a traditionally popular time for people to go shopping for cars. Often if a car is about to expire you don't get much choice about the timing of the sale you just need to get rid of it.

Can you afford it? Doing your sums again, what is the shortfall between what you can expect for your car and the amount you want to spend on the replacement?

So you want to sell a car do you? Well, there's more to it than simply writing an ad then sitting back and waiting for eager buyers to beat a path to your door. Get it wrong and there will be a monument on your drive. Get it right though and you can quickly move on to the next car.

CLEAN IT!: It's a fact: scruffy and smelly cars don't sell. Now cleaning the car you are about to sell sounds really obvious, but many forget to do the basics. Make the time to give the car a clean and not only will it be easier to sell you may be able to ask for and get a higher price. To buyers a car that is clean looks like it has been cared for.

So without going into huge detail simply vacuum and polish the interior then wash and wax the bodywork. Of course there is the option of getting the car professionally valeted. That saves you time and elbow grease, but it eats into your profit. If you are lazy just go down to the local car wash and the jet wash option is money well spent. Fine detailing on a classic or luxury car may be helpful, but on the vast majority of models it really isn't necessary. Also a car that is over prepared can put buyers off. Indeed, too much polishing will actually make scratches stand out. However, cleaning the car yourself makes you aware of exactly what needs to be fixed.

BODYWORK: Minor car park scrapes and thumbnail sized dents are not a problem, especially if the car is over five years old. As it is a Banger you can get away without spending on what will be expensive bodywork repairs. Big turn offs for buyers (well those who don't understand the whole concept of Bangernomics) are missing bits of trim and door mirrors. A trip to the salvage yard to pick up these items is absolutely essential. Make sure that all the doors and tailgate/boot open and close easily. A squirt of silicone lubricant will shut up any squeaks and the odd buzz or flap could be some loose trim, so tighten the screws.

Do: Fix and or replace broken trim. Make sure doors can be opened easily/quietly.
Don't: Buff black bumpers to a high gloss, or over polish bodywork or worry about parking/supermarket dents, it's a used car.

ENGINE: Every buyer wants to look under the bonnet even if they don't know what's going on in there. Buyers expect to see a tidy but honestly grimy unit. Don't be tempted to pressure wash because you could kill the electrics and you put buyers off who are suspicious of a shiny engine, it may even suggest that a serious oil leak is being hidden. By all means clean the oil filler cap and water expansion tank. Those are the things a buyer will touch and check so it looks to the buyer like the current owner (you) did that too. Indeed why not change the oil?

Make sure that the battery is secure and not caked in corrosion. Oh yes the bonnet stay should be there, or the hydraulic supports should work as it would be a bad idea for a buyer to bump their head. As for the engine, well if it isn't broken, don't even attempt to fix it. Ideally it should start first time, run evenly and quietly whilst squeaks can often be traced to loose belts.

Do: Check fluid levels, battery condition, bonnet opening, and make sure that the engine is running smoothly.
Don't: Pressure wash, or brighten up by polishing under the bonnet.

INTERIOR: Like we said, smells don't sell. If the car has been home to a smoker or a dog then you will have to work hard to get a neutral aroma. Vacuum and scrub away at the ashtray, clean head lining and wash or even replace the floor mats. Clean the dashboard, but don't be tempted to get a gloss finish. Overall, depersonalise the car because people don't want to see holiday stickers and football team badges, or what you enjoy snacking on. The boot may have more stains so use a carpet cleaning solution and take the opportunity to make sure that the tool kit is there and that the spare is usable and inflated.

Do: Get rid of smells, personal items and use domestic carpet cleaners.
Don't: Buff dashboard to a high shine or leave your personal effects and crisp packets lying around.

WHEELS/TYRES: You can be certain that buyers will kick these, so look at their condition. Alloy wheel refurbishment is costly, but lots of parking scrapes and chips on a very young car looks bad. Otherwise they should just be clean. Missing wheel trims instantly make any car look scruffy and should be replaced, often you can find them by the side of the road, but they are unlikely to match. Even the least clued up buyer can spot illegally worn tread and you must not sell an unroadworthy vehicle. Worst of all don't cheer old tyres up with a lick of tyre paint, it looks very tacky.

Do: Replace illegal tyres and replace missing wheel trims.
Don't: Use tyre paint.

GET ORGANISED: You have got the car sorted, but one of the most crucial parts of used car preparation is getting all the documentation in order. Indeed you can't put a car in your name without the registration/ownership document and any used car without this piece of paper can become worthless. Buyers like to see the paperwork neatly presented and not in a chaotic torn and tatty envelope. Get a clean file and clip in the registration document, the most recent roadworthiness certificate if applicable, the owner's manual in a clear wallet, plus any invoices for work done and especially any relevant warranties.

SETTING THE PRICE: How much is that doggie in the window? As rigidly defined areas of uncertainty go, valuing a car is difficult and really takes the dog biscuit. The mistake that most sellers make is to price their car too high, which frightens buyers away. Despite what they may say, everyone buys on price. Consult price guides and most importantly look at the adverts for cars local to you. More importantly, price your car according to where you are advertising it because it will be compared against similar vehicles.

ADVERTISING: There is an art to writing an effective motoring ad. It is crucial to get the wording right, otherwise you won't get a response and if you do, it won't necessarily be the right sort. The purpose of the advertisement is not so much to fully describe the car as to get interested parties to contact you and buy it. In this digital age there is no end to the amount you could write which is no bad thing. Also the number of pictures you can upload can be limitless, again not a bad thing at all.

The 10 most important elements are:

Year registered: So the buyer knows exactly which model.

Service history: If you've got it, flaunt it. 'FSH' (full service history) is an accepted abbreviation.

Mileage: Be specific if the car has a low mileage. Mileage becomes less of an issue as the car gets older and can be dropped if you are flogging a banger, but buyers still like to know.

Model: This is vitally important in a marketplace that places emphasis on differences between an L and GL. Buyers also want to know the engine size, so 1.6, 2.0, diesel and whether the gearbox is automatic. Don't waste words on the specification if it costs you more, if not list absolutely everything.

Colour: A crucial buying factor to many people, a picture ad may be too small and blurry, so say what it is.

Condition: Honesty really is the best policy. If there is a major fault, then mention it. 'Good condition, but gearbox needs attention hence …' that lovely word 'hence' qualifies the defect and justifies a lower than normal price.

Price: The word 'offers' or 'ono' (or near offer) at the end of the description is wrong because it indicates that you are desperate to sell at any price. Buyers always make an offer anyway.

Contact Details: Sounds obvious, but a phone number, email or whatever form of communication we may use in the future which may include telepathy, is always going to help.

Number of Owners: If you have been the only custodian, or there have been few owners in the last decade, this is another reassuring indicator for the potential purchaser.

Warranties: Any existing guarantees, or warranties for parts, or recent repairs.

Do: Stick to the facts.
Don't: Use superlatives and exaggerations, they can backfire.

DEALING WITH BUYERS

Like it or not, the grumpy so and so kicking the tyres is a valued customer. Treat him/her as such and you stand a better chance of selling the car, but always stay in charge of the situation. Answer any questions on the phone, by email, or in person directly and don't flannel. If you are honest and straightforward you are more likely to hook a potential buyer. When it comes to making an appointment don't allow yourself to be trapped into an inconvenient time, or become a prisoner in the house waiting for someone to put in an appearance. Always take the enquirer's contact details and then call back to make the final arrangements so you know they are genuine. Most of all never make the appointment late in the evening, or agree to take your car to a venue that could leave you vulnerable. Ideally if you are the nervous type or just concerned, ensure that a friend or relative will be with you at all times.

When the buyer arrives be friendly and helpful and because you are not desperate to sell this car, don't fuss around the buyer, or talk too much. Simply ensure that all the doors are unlocked, raise the bonnet and leave the buyer to it, but don't leave the keys with them! Then retire gracefully to prod at the garden, stay in the vicinity, but let the buyer look around. Don't offer to do anything, like start the car or go for a drive. If they are interested then they will ask, if not they may simply go along with your offers to keep you happy and that is a waste of everyone's time. Also, leaving them alone with the car makes it less likely that they will criticise it and put you on the defensive.

TEST DRIVE: If the buyer wants a drive the most important thing to remember is that you should remain in control at all times. Often your insurance can cover other drivers provided you give your permission, but do you honestly want to jeopardise your policy? Make it clear that if someone wants to drive, they have to be comprehensively covered for your vehicle and you will have to see a valid insurance policy and driving licence as proof. Remember if someone doesn't have the right insurance cover, or you just don't fancy them driving, don't ever let them.

THE DRIVE: Make sure that you drive first. This is so you can show that the car can be driven smoothly and there are no problems with a crunchy gearbox, juddering brakes and sluggish performance. Drive to a quiet road and invite the potential buyer to take the wheel. But before they do that, take the keys with you, or they could take the car. Make sure that they are comfortable. Explain the controls.

Specify a local route, avoid built up areas and school run snarl-ups. Chat freely during the drive, point things out that you think are relevant. Don't babble on. Silence often provokes favourable responses from the driver.

AFTER THE DRIVE: Remain in the car and ask if the buyer has any questions and as they have looked, touched, prodded and driven it is not unreasonable to ask whether they want to buy. If they do, go somewhere more comfortable like your house and make a cuppa.

THE DEAL: Be polite, low-key, helpful, never get excited and never show that you are desperate. Being chatty ought to help when it comes to the negotiations. If the buyer makes an offer be prepared to drop in price to half of the difference, but not until you have been asked, never give anything away for nothing. Don't babble because this gives away too much information and weakens your position. Always link your acceptance of any offer with a condition, such as payment within a set period. If the buyer does not bite then tell them that's the deal take it or leave it. Being polite means that the door remains open if the buyer wants to reconsider. If the buyer is keen to buy, but does not have the funds to pay in full then get a deposit in cash. It concentrates the buyer's mind wonderfully and stops them having second thoughts, or simply walking away just leaving a promise behind.

WEAK?: If you think that you are a weakling when it comes to negotiation then why not nominate a friend, or hard-nosed spouse to do the difficult bit? After showing the buyer around the car and doing the test-drive, then 'hand over' the

SELLING: GOLDEN RULE NO.4

DURING NEGOTIATION BE FIRM, FAIR AND FRIENDLY

buyer with an 'I've got no head for figures, my friend/spouse/dog handles all that'. This is a technique used by showrooms, which softens up customers with a nice salesman and then squeezes out the cash with a nasty one.

GOLDEN RULE: Never stop taking enquiries until you have been paid in full for the car. The potential buyer could drop out and you will then have a list of numbers from people who have responded to your brilliantly worded advertisement, to fall back on. Never under any circumstances accept more than one deposit, as you will get yourself into legal hot water and possibly a black eye.

SOLD!: Once you have shaken hands, the hard part is getting the money. You should also put the agreement into formal terms, even though an oral contract usually exists once you have agreed the price.

DEPOSIT: Insist on cash; it concentrates the buyer's mind on your car. A cheque can be cancelled and a promise of payment isn't always fulfilled. A customer with second thoughts, or suddenly finding another car that takes their fancy, can soon fail to come up with the readies. Without a deposit, there is no intention to purchase and no good faith. Specify that it is non-refundable. Don't believe someone who says that don't have any cash on them, as no one goes to buy a car without money. They have to give you cash or the car remains for sale. Simple.

RECEIPT: To acknowledge the money you should give the buyer a receipt and whilst you are at it, put the details of the deal on paper. Keep it simple, write down the facts about the car (registration, colour, make), the parties (you and the buyer), the sale price and amount of deposit. The BanGlossary should help.

TERMS: The important part is for the car to be 'sold as seen', or 'sold as seen tried and approved' as you are not guaranteeing that it will be fault free for two years or anything stupid like that. Should the car be sold for spares, again make this clear as you could be prosecuted for selling an unroadworthy car. Any conditions that you have agreed should also be included. So if you've put the onus on the buyer to take the car the next day and pay in full, put this in the contract. If you've agreed to have the car tuned, again be specific otherwise the buyer could ask for a full service. Then both parties sign. Make sure you have a copy.

DON'T: This seems obvious, but don't hand over any documentation, or the car, until you have received full payment. Some unsavoury characters have asked to borrow registration documents when in fact they want to use it to sell a stolen vehicle of the same make. Don't keep all the documents in the glove compartment, or show the buyer where you keep them. Never let someone take the car away 'to show their mum', even though they don't have the registration documents it won't stop them selling it elsewhere, or nicking all the best bits.

CASH: The best way to get paid, especially if it is a relatively small amount. Always count the amount, as buyers make mistakes, not always innocently, and get someone else to double-check it, especially if the denominations are small. If you are nervous about receiving money arrange to take it at a bank. The cashier will count it and be able to spot a forgery very quickly. Also some nasty buyers just want to show you the money and take the car with a bit of violence. So a bank is a safe place to do the exchange. BANKER'S DRAFT: Effectively this is the bank's own cheque and is as good as cash and is the only other fool/full proof way of accepting payment on the day of delivery. There are though forgeries and when in doubt contact the Bank. CHEQUE: Never take a personal cheque, unless you clear it first (usually three to five working days), or pay for special clearance.

DIRECT TRANSFER: It is possible to send money directly to your bank account online. See the BANGLOSSARY chapter for a sample sale/deposit agreement. To sum up, get cash, but again money can be forged. Always find out from your government what the latest guidelines are to spot a forgery in your currency.

Alternatively ...

SELLING TO THE CAR TRADE: There are dealers seemingly desperate to buy your old car, but the problem is they want to pay a 'trade' price. The advantage is that you get a quick decision and instant cash without the hassle of trying to sell privately. The normal rules apply so that you should clean and prepare the car and have all the documentation ready.

AUCTIONS: Just as hassle free, but again cars are usually sold at 'trade prices' or less. You will also pay an entry fee and a percentage on the sale price. If you are lucky a bidder could possibly pay more than it is worth, but don't bank on it. There are of course online auctions, see back for how to buy which will also give you guidance on how to sell.

SCRAP: If your car has been pronounced unroadworthy or has died mechanically you may get the scrap value, or even a token amount depending on the value of metal at the time. Some specialist breakers yards may pay extra for an obscure or rare model. Also contact owners' clubs who may be able to make use of the parts and may take the car away for free. Ensure though they will dispose of the car responsibly, that may seem difficult, but maybe ask for proof (a receipt) that it has been done, otherwise the car could be traced back to you and you could be made liable for any laws that have been broken.

INCREDIBLE HULK: Potential buyers have sniggered, a dealer offered a derisory sum and the neighbours have got up a petition for its removal. Your pride and joy isn't going anywhere, so what do you do? The simple answer may be to chop it into bits. But instead of giving those bits to the dustmen you can actually sell them off individually. The fact is that most Bangers are worth more in bits than they are in one piece. OPTION 1: If you have the space, store the vehicle away and remove the pieces as you sell them. OPTION 2: Remove the most saleable items from the car and store those away for sale. One reason for keeping the old Banger is if you buy an almost identical replacement then you have your own parts store for free. Just make sure that the car isn't an unsightly hulk, rotting in your garden.

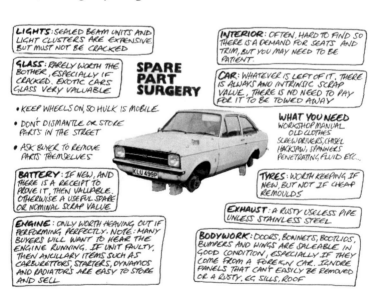

SPARE PART SURGERY

LIGHTS: SEALED BEAM UNITS AND LIGHT CLUSTERS ARE EXPENSIVE BUT MUST NOT BE CRACKED

GLASS: RARELY WORTH THE BOTHER, ESPECIALLY IF CRACKED. EXOTIC CARS GLASS VERY VALUABLE

• KEEP WHEELS ON, SO HULK IS MOBILE

• DON'T DISMANTLE OR STORE PARTS IN THE STREET

• ASK BUYER TO REMOVE PARTS THEMSELVES

BATTERY: IF NEW, AND THERE IS A RECEIPT TO PROVE IT, THEN VALUABLE. OTHERWISE A USEFUL SPARE OR NOMINAL SCRAP VALUE

ENGINE: ONLY WORTH HEAVING OUT IF PERFORMING PERFECTLY. NOTE: MANY BUYERS WILL WANT TO HEAR THE ENGINE RUNNING. IF UNIT FAULTY, THEN ANCILLARY ITEMS SUCH AS CARBURETTORS, STARTERS, DYNAMOS AND RADIATORS ARE EASY TO STORE AND SELL

INTERIOR: OFTEN, HARD TO FIND SO THERE IS A DEMAND FOR SEATS AND TRIM, BUT YOU MAY NEED TO BE PATIENT.

CAR: WHATEVER IS LEFT OF IT. THERE IS ALWAYS AN INTRINSIC SCRAP VALUE, THERE IS NO NEED TO PAY FOR IT TO BE TOWED AWAY

WHAT YOU NEED WORKSHOP MANUAL OLD CLOTHES SCREWDRIVERS, CHISEL HACKSAW, SPANNERS PENETRATING FLUID ETC...

TYRES: WORTH KEEPING IF NEW, BUT NOT IF CHEAP REMOULDS

EXHAUST: A RUSTY USELESS PIPE UNLESS STAINLESS STEEL

BODYWORK: DOORS, BONNETS, BOOTLIDS, BUMPERS AND WINGS ARE SALEABLE IN GOOD CONDITION, ESPECIALLY IF THEY COME FROM A FOREIGN CAR. IGNORE PANELS THAT CAN'T EASILY BE REMOVED OR A RUSTY, EG SILLS, ROOF

KLU 499P

WHAT YOU NEED: Most basic tool kits have the necessary items to reduce a vehicle to its constituent parts: spanners; a socket set; pliers; wrenches; cutters; a hammer; chisels; hacksaw; releasing fluid/penetrating oil; and don't forget to don old clothes. Power tools can sometimes speed up the process, but they are not strictly necessary. A workshop manual could also save you inflicting unnecessary damage on a part you want to salvage, but we told you to get one of those ages ago. Dispose of all fluids and other unsold parts responsibly, as a recycling yard will be pleased to take metal and old oil.

Bye Bye Banger – Coursework

You know a lot about buying cars so put that to good use when it comes to selling. All those things you didn't enjoy about the buying experience you should try and put right. Write down how you could make the disposal/selling process easier for a potential buyer. Maybe you should not deal with the buyers because you haven't got the patience. Perhaps you will get your local garage to agree to give a report on the car's roadworthiness. Maybe you put together a highly detailed photo album or video film. I dunno, anything unusual could help you sell, try and be different.

13

A to B to Z of Bangers

*Which really means contact
Bangernomics.com for Free Lifetime Support*

JUST ABOUT HERE IN the original Bangernomics book I used to list loads of cars from the '60s onwards and although I tried really hard it was never going to be a comprehensive listing of all past, present and potential Bangers. Indeed, I may have started a few arguments. There is now of course the Interweb, which has a huge network of owners' clubs and forums that can provide inside information on every make and model of car ever. My own prejudiced, often juvenile opinions are based on a lifetime of mixed motoring experiences, driving disappointments and numerous ill-advised purchases and sales. All I can do as an act of Bangernomic good faith is to provide you with lifetime support. Initially it will be my lifetime, however long that turns out to be, although I will try and sort something out in the far flung future for PTDs. That's Personal Transportation Devices as absolutely no one is ever going to call whatever replaces cars. So while emails and the Internet exist you can contact me (for as long I exist) for biased advice through the Bangernomics.com website, or whatever clever interactive technology replaces it.

Good luck, because you are going to need it.

14

Banglossary

Checklists etc

HERE THEY ARE, ALL the crib sheets, checklists and standard forms you will need to help you become fully qualified in the science of Bangernomics. There may be more information on it than you need, but it is a fairly simple checklist which will help you calculate quickly whether the Banger you want to buy is a good one. So if you are applying more crosses than ticks, it might be worth looking at another Banger.

Don't get too hung up on testing everything, especially if you are not sure what an exhaust is and exactly where the petrol tank may be. If something looks wrong then make a note for yourself and ask an expert later.

Because we are so generous the author and publishers (which is basically just me) grant permission to the purchaser of this book/course to make copies of these lists for your own private Bangernomic buying purposes. Please don't copy them to resell or redistribute and ideally if you have a friend who is interested in Bangernomics, ask them to buy the book. I'd really appreciate that.

I am obliged to issue a disclaimer that these lists and forms are not comprehensive and we take no responsibility for how you use these materials and we can't guarantee that if you use these lists you will buy a brilliant Banger. However, we do think that these will probably help, a bit.

GENERAL GUIDELINES
ACCIDENT?: If body panels have been repaired, the paint-work looks patchy and has different textures, you can see repairs or welds in the engine bay, boot area or underneath.

FAKED IDENTITY?: VIN (vehicle identification number) plate fitted in engine bay and on dashboard tampered with, windows and lights and all glass with scratched off areas, stickers over etching, or documentation does not match the car.

CLOCKED?: Mileometer figures out of line, condition inconsistent with indicated mileage, mileage on service documents very different from indicated mileage, documentation missing. High mileage is not necessarily a problem, but if the seller has lied about this, or altered the mileage in any way, what else have they changed on the car without telling you?

STOLEN?: Documents inconsistent with owner or car details, registration plate changed, VIN plates tampered with, or documents do not look genuine.

VEHICLE DETAILS
Get these from the car itself so that you can compare them with the documentation supplied with the car.

Make/Model _____

Year _____

Colour _____

Registration_____

VIN_____

Engine No _____

Mileage _____

DOCUMENT CHECK: Take your time and carefully look at all the paperwork, if any is missing ask where they are.

MOT/Annual Check/Roadworthiness Certificate_____
Does it look genuine, does it match other details on the car?

Registration/Ownership Document_____
Does it look genuine, does it match other details on the car?

Warranties_____
Are there any relating to tyres, the car etc? Ask.

Tax_____
Does the tax disc belong to the car?

Insurance_____
Are there any documents, do they match the car/owner?

Last Service_____ Cam belt change _____
Is there any service history?

BODY CHECK Use the flat drawing of the car to identify any damage and also this key will help. Tick or cross as appropriate and then make any comments

key F = front **R** = rear **D** = damage **C** = corrosion **O** or circle = repairs

A tick in the box means the item is satisfactory, an **X** indicates that there is a problem that you might want to make a comment on.

door locks   ☐
door mirrors   ☐
exterior trim   ☐
fuel filler cover/ cap   ☐
glass   ☐
number plates   ☐
paintwork   ☐
soft top operation   ☐

WHEEL/TYRE CHECK

tyre front left ☐
tyre front right ☐
tyre rear left ☐
tyre rear right ☐
wheel rims ☐
wheel trims ☐

LIGHTS/WIPERS CHECK

(You will need a friend to
help you with the lights)
auxiliary lights ☐
headlamp washer ☐
headlamp wiper ☐
headlights ☐
indicators/hazards ☐
number plate light ☐
rear lights ☐
reverse/fog lights ☐
side lights ☐
stop lights ☐
wipers/washers ☐

ENGINE CHECK When cold.

bonnet operation ☐
coolant level ☐
drive belts ☐
engine oil level ☐
brake fluid level ☐
clutch fluid ☐
hoses/pipes ☐
cold starting ☐
fumes/smoke ☐
noise level (cold) ☐
oil leaks ☐
steering fluid ☐

INTERIOR CHECKS Use the
interior plan.

adjustable mirrors ☐
air conditioning ☐
boot lock ☐
carpets ☐
central locking ☐
cigarette lighter /socket ☐
door locking ☐
door seals/hinges ☐
door trim ☐
headlining ☐
heater fan/controls ☐
ignition lock ☐
illumination lights ☐
interior sills ☐
luggage area ☐
mirrors ☐
panel lights ☐
rear parcel shelf ☐
seat belts ☐
seat mechanism ☐
seat trim front ☐
seat trim rear ☐
sound system ☐
spare wheel ☐
steering adjustment ☐
sunroof ☐
switches/controls ☐
tool kit ☐
windows ☐

UNDERSIDE CHECK: Don't get underneath, don't use a jack, just see what you can from just getting down on the ground. Use the underside picture. Look for any damage, obvious leaks and corrosion that you should mark with a (C). This is a visual check of course and not a mechanical assessment.

oil leaks ☐
pipes/hoses ☐
suspension ☐

EXHAUST CHECK
joints/couplings ☐
mountings ☐
pipes ☐
silencer(s) ☐

TRANSMISSION CHECK
fluid/oil leaks ☐
mountings ☐

FUEL CHECK
fuel lines ☐
leaks ☐
tank ☐

BRAKE CHECK
discs/pads ☐
flexible hoses ☐
fluid leaks ☐
pedal/linkage ☐
pipes/connections ☐

TEST DRIVE CHECK: Make sure you are insured and bear the following points in mind. The car should start easily. The oil and ignition light should go out quickly. It should pull away smoothly without any strange noises, and not jump out of gear or perform sluggishly. Pull away on a hill, the handbrake should hold the car and the clutch, if the car is a manual, should hold the car on the hill. On the descent look out for blue smoke. If you can, try an emergency stop on a clear quiet road. The car must not pull to one side and the brakes should not squeal. The steering should not wander if you release your grip on the steering wheel. Over rough ground the car must not pitch too much and listen out for banging noises. When cornering there ought to be no knocks, clonks or clicks, or general rumbling from the wheels. On a dual carriageway listen out for and feel for vibration. An automatic gearbox should change smoothly.

4wd operation	☐
clutch	☐
engine noise	☐
engine	☐
excess smoke	☐
footbrake	☐
gearbox	☐
hand/park brake	☐
hot restarting	☐
controls	☐
overheating	☐
road holding	☐
steering	☐
suspension noise	☐
warning lights	☐

AFTER THE DRIVE: With the engine running look for oil leaks in the engine bay, any leaks from the hoses and smoke coming from the oil filter if you can see it.

Should you get as far as actually buying then here is a receipt and holding deposit templates you can use and adapt. As ever this is not a legally binding document, but it may help you collate evidence if there is a dispute.

BANGERNOMICS RECEIPT

I.. (SELLER'S NAME)

of ....

....

(ADDRESS) confirm that I am the owner of the vehicle

MAKE..

....

MODEL..

REGISTRATION ....

(or that I am authorised to sell it on behalf of the owner)

NAME..

ADDRESS..

I confirm that the vehicle does not have any faults which I have
not disclosed/and that the recorded mileage of ....
is correct. I agree to:

....

.... before sale.

(DETAIL REPAIRS)

HOLDING DEPOSIT I _____ (SELLER'S NAME)
accept the sum of £ .... as a holding deposit on the above
vehicle, which is fully returnable provided a decision is made
within ____ days/ hours. The purchase price for the above vehicle
will be £.................

SIGNED...

DATE...

15

Bangernomics Proficiency Certificate

Read the book, buy a Banger and get some letters after your name.

PLEASED WITH THE BANGER you've bought? Delighted with how wonderful it is to drive? Can't contain your glee at just how super it is? Then tell us all about it at Bangernomics.com and most importantly send us some pictures (you with the book and the car) and we will issue you with a Bangercertificate. How wonderful is that? Plus you can officially put the letters B.A.N.G.E.R (Bought A New Groovy Economical Runabout) after your name. Or you can just cheat and tear this one out and put it on your wall.

For the latest details on how to claim your certificate, please go to bangernomics.com.

BANGERNOMICS

Proficiency Certificate

This is to certify that....................... is proficient in Bangernomics

James Ruppert

The Back

Goodbye and good luck out there and remember,
always beware of the dog.

Lightning Source UK Ltd.
Milton Keynes UK
15 March 2010

151425UK00001B/68/P